Twenty20 Cricket

HOW TO PLAY, COACH AND WIN

Twenty20 Cricket

HOW TO PLAY, COACH AND WIN

Matt Homes & Darren Talbot

Published in the UK in 2011 by
John Wisden & Co
An imprint of Bloomsbury Publishing Plc
36 Soho Square, London W1D 3QY
www.wisden.com
www.bloomsbury.com

Copyright © Matt Homes, Darren Talbot 2011
Chapter five copyright © Kieron Vorster 2011

ISBN 978 1 4081 2914 2

All rights reserved. No part of this publication may be reproduced in any form or by any means – graphic, electronic or mechanical, including photocopying, recording, taping or information storage and retrieval systems – without the prior permission in writing of the publishers.

Matt Homes and Darren Talbot have asserted their right under the Copyright, Design and Patents Act, 1988, to be identified as the authors of this work.

A CIP catalogue record for this book is available from the British Library.

Commissioned by Charlotte Atyeo
Edited by Rebecca Senior
Designed by Greg Stevenson
Cover photograph © Getty Images
Photographs on pages 7, 8, 9, 19, 20, 23, 28, 29, 40, 43, 49, 53, 57, 62, 64, 69, 70, 72, 73, 81, 83, 92, 93, 95, 97, 99, 100, 105, 106, 107 © Getty Images
All other photographs © Grant Pritchard
Illustrations on pages 129 to 135 by JB Illustrations
Illustrations on pages 122 to 128 by Greg Stevenson

This book is produced using paper that is made from wood grown in managed, sustainable forests. It is natural, renewable and recyclable. The logging and manufacturing processes conform to the environmental regulations of the country of origin.

Typeset in 11 point Minion by Saxon Graphics Ltd, Derby

Printed and bound in Great Britain by Martins the Printers

CONTENTS

Introduction	1
PART 1: BATTING	**3**
1. Power hit	8
2. Shimmy / using feet to pace and spin	12
3. Low full toss / yorker-length striking	15
4. Manipulating the ball	18
5. Pick-up shot	22
6. Uppercut	25
7. Slog sweep	29
8. Paddle sweep	33
9. Reverse sweep	36
10. Dilscoop / lap shot	40
11. Front-on squat lap shot	43
12. Switch hit	46
13. Front-foot pull / hook	49
14. Running between the wickets	52
PART 2: BOWLING	**55**
15. Changing pace: slower balls	59
16. Varying your length: yorkers	64
17. Bowling cross-seam	67
18. Bowling at the death	69
19. Bowling spin	72

PART 3: FIELDING — 75

20. Retrieve / stop and drag back — 78
21. Stop / flick-back slide (hunt in pairs) — 81
22. Slide interception — 83
23. Roll-over interception — 85
24. Diving slide — 87
25. One-handed pick-up, side-arm throw — 89
26. Diving catching — 92
27. Diving forward catch — 95
28. Catching on the move — 97
29. High boundary flick-back catch — 99
30. Backing up — 102

PART 4: WICKETKEEPING — 103

31. Standing back — 106
32. Standing up to the seamers — 108

PART 5: FITNESS — 111

33. Physical testing — 114
34. Drills — 121
35. Exercises — 129

ACKNOWLEDGEMENTS

The authors wish to thank the following for their help and support in putting this book together.

Kieron Vorster is a REPS advanced instructor level 3 strength and conditioning coach. He has previously worked as a personal fitness coach for both Tim Henman and Wayne Ferreira, and as the head of strength and conditioning for the Lawn Tennis Association. He is the strength and conditioning consultant for the In-Touch Cricket Academy, and contributed to part 5 of this book.

Ben Scott, a high-quality keeper/batsman, has played for Middlesex (who won the Twenty20 Cup in 2008), Worcestershire, Surrey and the England Lions. Ben teaches cricket skills and runs strength and conditioning sessions for the In-Touch Cricket Academy. He has demonstrated many of the shots described in this book, and contributed to the section on wicketkeeping.

The authors also wish to thank England Women's player Ebony Rainsford-Brent, Tom Homes and Aamir Nazir for their invaluable assistance in modelling the shots that have been used throughout this book. Our thanks go to Epsom College for kindly allowing us to take our photographs in their sports hall.

AUTHORS' NOTE

The models used in our photographs to demonstrate some of the batting shots appear without helmets. In this instance we used tennis balls rather than hard balls, and confident, skilled players when taking these photographs. Please note: we would always recommend the use of helmets when working with young or inexperienced players. This also applies to many of the wicketkeeping drills.

TWENTY20: AN INTRODUCTION

Over the last decade, Twenty20 cricket has taken over the world and is now one of the most popular forms of the game, even though there are still some purists who find it difficult to accept!

With this new form of the game has come innovation, and in this book we will look at some of these new ideas, skills and techniques and show you how you can use them in your 20-over matches to become a better limited-overs cricketer.

What we won't be covering are the everyday batting shots and strategies that are commonplace in cricket. Don't assume because they don't feature that they shouldn't be used, however. Indeed the skills you already have are, and should remain, the cornerstone of your cricket armoury.

As well as explaining the skills and strategies of Twenty20 cricket, we will show you how to combat them if you're on the opposing team. We'll also give you some mental and physical tips on how to become your club's best Twenty20 cricketer.

Being a multi-faceted cricketer is becoming ever more important in this form of the game. If you are a good batter who becomes a reliable close or boundary fielder, or can slip in a couple of overs, as Kevin Pietersen often does in Twenty20 cricket, that could make you an invaluable player. Similarly, big strong fast bowlers are typically not the most agile around the field, but if you can work on your fielding and fitness to the point where you can save an extra 5–10 runs, you can make up for that over where they took you for 20 – not an unusual occurrence in Twenty20 cricket.

Never stop working at your game, whatever your role in the team. And most of all – enjoy your cricket.

PART ONE

BATTING

INTRODUCTION

In this chapter we will look at a number of different shots and techniques batters can use in Twenty20 cricket. But first, we should look at the general approach to batting in 20-over cricket.

GAME PLAN

So what is a good score in Twenty20 cricket? Well, that depends on a number of factors: the pitch, the conditions, and the strengths and weaknesses of your team – and your opponents' team – to name but a few.

One thing is for sure, though. Losing a block of wickets early in your innings can severely handicap your ability to reach a competitive total or chase down a score.

It is important that a good positive mental attitude and body language is maintained whatever the onfield situation, as this helps waiting batters.

As a general rule, in most forms of cricket, especially colts cricket, 120 is about the minimum score you need to be competitive batting first against evenly matched teams in average conditions. A score of 120 is often defendable and, although lower totals are not always losing ones, you are going to have to work incredibly hard as a bowling and fielding unit to come away with a victory.

Around 150, however, is more like a competitive score. In the 2010 Indian Premier League (IPL) series, the average score in the 60 matches played was 146, with a lowest of 71 and a highest of 246.

POWERPLAY BATTING

With only two fielders outside the 30-yard inner ring for the first six overs of an innings, batters do not need to slog or take that many unnecessary risks.

The condition of the pitch and how much the new ball is doing will dictate the amount of risk that can be taken to a degree. In England the ball is likely to move around a bit more early on, so it may pay to be slightly more cautious; in other countries the ball may not do so much, and taking risks can be profitable.

Batters need to bear in mind, though, that it will be easier to hit the ball further in the first few overs while it is still new and hard, whereas when it loses its shine and gets softer in the later stages, it may become more difficult to clear the fence.

Although batters will potentially look to hit the ball over the infield during this passage of play, more orthodox cricketing shots can also be utilised by manoeuvring the ball with control. If the gaps in the field are exploited, you will get more value for your shots by more frequently running twos – or with the ball running away to the boundary if the shot is timed well.

Teams sometimes pair up a hitter with a grafter at the top of the innings. The hitter will have licence to strike out during the powerplay overs, with the grafter expected to ensure that the hitter gets as much strike as possible. As a back-up, teams may well have a hitter and grafter padded up to replace the batter of their own type if they get out, to ensure that this game plan continues throughout the powerplay.

This obviously highlights the need for a good all-round range of proper cricketing shots. Getting off to a good start in Twenty20 is important so, as well as looking to hit boundaries, regular rotation of the strike is crucial to avoid pressure building and a big 'out' shot.

A good total in the powerplay overs is ideally somewhere between 45 and 55 runs, losing no more than two wickets. Wickets in hand for the remaining 14 overs, in which a maximum of five fielders can be outside the ring, must be taken into account, although becoming too cautious with a low run-rate can obviously build pressure on incoming batters.

The mental approach may well differ if you are chasing a big total where you have to go out hard and hit boundaries.

The balance of the opening pair, and of numbers 3 and 4, could well be a consideration in selection for the powerplay overs. There are currently many destructive opening partnerships in the IPL Twenty20 with the likes of Virender Sehwag and David Warner, Adam Gilchrist and Herschelle Gibbs; however, one of the most successful partnerships shown by the statistics below – Rahul Dravid and Jacques Kallis – represents the more traditional batters. Another highly successful batter in the IPL is the great Sachin Tendulkar, who is both intelligent and inventive in his approach.

Powerplays / IPL 2010

Team	Avge runs scored	Avge wkts lost
Sehwag/Warner	51.21	2.00
Kallis/Dravid	45.38	0.94
Gilchrist/Gibbs	44.69	1.94

BATTING IN THE MIDDLE OVERS

After the initial powerplay overs, if wickets remain intact, there is licence to continue batting in very much the same vein. If it's going well, why change it?

If wickets have been lost, the middle overs become more about setting the team up for a final onslaught in the last three or four overs. It is possible to achieve 40–50 runs off the last four overs, especially with wickets in hand, so it's important not to go for all-out attack in the middle overs if early wickets have fallen.

Having said that, it is equally important that runs don't dry up altogether in the middle overs. The innings needs to retain momentum to ensure the fielding side don't get the upper hand. The section on manipulating the ball (see page 18) covers some ideas on how to do this.

When chasing, it is better to keep in touch with the required run rate as much as possible. Although 40 or 50 runs off the last four overs is achievable, you don't really want to be leaving yourself this sort of run rate as a matter of course. Try to keep up with the rate as near as possible during the middle overs and leave less to do at the end.

A SHORT NOTE ABOUT BAT WEIGHT

In professional cricket, most batters will use a different bat for Twenty20 cricket. Some select a heavier bat for 'smashing it', some go lighter for a quicker bat speed. Others are using new innovation bats such as the long-handled, short-bladed Mongoose.

Hayden using the Mongoose bat

It is very much personal preference as to what weight bat you use for Twenty20 cricket – that's assuming you have a choice! If you are able to access a range of bat weights, practise with different ones and see what effect it has on your game. Most of all, make sure you are comfortable with your choice when you're out in the middle.

The England batsman Paul Collingwood turned himself into more of a hitter in Twenty20 cricket by practising range hitting with a specially designed 5lb bat. This made it easier for him to clear the boundary with his normal bat when it came to match play.

POWER HIT

Striking from a strong base is at the heart of the majority of shots played in Twenty20. If you can master how to strike a ball cleanly from a solid base, you open up an array of run-scoring opportunities all around the wicket.

This is probably the most fundamental shot for Twenty20 cricket and encompasses many other shots.

In days gone by this may well have been referred to as a 'slog' if hit towards wide mid-wicket, but these days we can refer to it as a power hit. The front leg is cleared out of the way to allow the ball to be hit into this area. However, there is much more to this shot than swinging wildly – a base can be created to enable you to hit the ball into many more areas, as we will demonstrate.

In the Twenty20 format you need to hit big runs, essentially striking the ball for four (or ideally six) as often as the bowling allows. It is just as appropriate throughout the innings as it is during the early powerplay overs or at the death. Twenty overs pass very quickly and you don't want too many overs of singles and twos. You will soon fall behind the necessary scoring rate that way.

HOW TO PLAY IT

What you are looking for is a *length delivery*. That is a ball that is in your half of the wicket and in the zone where your bat can get underneath it. This allows the elevation of the ball over the top, keeping the bat face through the line of the ball for as long as possible.

Receiving and preparing to hit the length delivery; note the solid base

It is effectively a front-foot shot that can be executed anywhere from a wide-stance position through to a more traditional front-foot drive position; your front foot, head and momentum will move towards the line of the ball, creating a strong base before the downswing of the bat commences.

How do you know when you have a strong base? If you've got it right you should feel as though you are perfectly balanced and that, if someone were to try to push you over, they would have great difficulty doing so. The knees have to be flexed, with good alignment of the feet, hips and shoulders to get this right.

From this base, with your foot coming towards the ball, your bat should continue the momentum by working your shoulders and arms vertically through the line of the ball, continuing on the same path without closing the face of the bat, and getting under the ball. You need to meet the ball slightly out in front of your body with the bat path past the vertical to get the necessary elevation to send it over the infield and sailing over the boundary.

Your head position is vitally important, as with all cricket shots – it should remain still and watching the ball throughout execution. This is particularly relevant when hitting the ball in the air on the on-side as the head has a tendency

Playing the shot

The shot struck with real impetus and the full face of the bat through the ball

to fall to the off-side and therefore it is important that the head stays still behind the line of the ball with the eyes remaining level at all times.

The shot can be struck in any direction from the extra cover region to wide mid-wicket, according to the line of the ball. Make sure you hit through the line of the ball and avoid trying to fetch a ball from outside offstump over mid-wicket. The shot is most effectively played through the same line with the hands working together keeping the bat face open after contact, through to either a check or full follow-through position.

TROUBLESHOOTING

- Don't lean back with your weight sinking into your back leg. Keep all your momentum towards your hitting target area.

- Don't try to hit the ball too hard, although good bat speed is really important in Twenty20 cricket.

- Make sure your bottom hand doesn't come in too early on the shot, closing the face of the bat.

- Don't lift your head too early to follow the trajectory of the ball.

- Don't choose the wrong ball! It's got to be a length delivery so play the ball rather than the situation.

- Find gaps in the field that provide some margin for error in case you do not make it over the boundary.

- Be positive. Back yourself to clear the boundary. Visualise the ball clearing the rope to increase confidence levels.

HOW TO PRACTISE IT

Beginner level
Start from the solid base position, ready to hit the ball. Initially the coach can drop feed the ball to the batter; then, as progress is made, move on to a bobble feed. Concentrate on watching the ball and striking it cleanly as far as possible.

Intermediate level
Start from the normal stance, stepping into the delivery, hitting towards a target area. The coach can use different-coloured balls to add an element of processing

information as though in a match situation. For example, a red ball will need to be hit through mid-wicket, a blue ball straight back past the bowler and a green ball over mid-off. The speed of feeds can also be increased for progression, making sure the batter continues to be aligned with the ball every shot. Thinking quickly and smartly is the key to Twenty20 cricket.

Advanced level

At this level a hard ball can be used, either with throw-downs or a bowling machine. The coach can call out where to target the shot as the ball is released, eg off-side or on-side – or you could number the different areas of a pitch and then call out the number. This can be tried from the base position and from a stance position. Another progression is to give rapid-fire feeds, which produce a pressure situation.

A simple and effective way to practise this is to stand in the middle with hard-ball throw-downs or bowlers and practise hitting sixes over the boundary – sometimes known as *range hitting*. This also helps you to visualise and feel what it's like for the ball to go over the boundary – 'train the brain!'

Fielding captain's note

The best way to combat this shot is for the bowler to change their length or vary their pace – or both (see pages 59–66).
  Make sure you set an appropriate field, bearing in mind that a well-executed shot will end up well over the boundary. During powerplays this could be particularly difficult, so you'll need to rely on bowlers being able to vary their length and pace in the first six overs.

SHIMMY / USING FEET TO PACE AND SPIN

During the course of an innings, batters need to make things happen to keep the run-rate ticking over. Too many dot balls can be the death knell of a Twenty20 innings. Using your feet with the shimmy, either to pace or spin bowlers, can help to get the score ticking over again.

The shimmy is the sort of shot you would look to play if things aren't going your way and you are slipping behind the rate. It is a *percentage* shot, and there is a risk element – it's not necessarily the sort of shot you would look to play early on in your innings, and ideally you should have wickets in hand.

What you are aiming to do is turn a shorter-length ball into a good-length one, and a good-length ball into a fuller-length one, bringing it within the striking area. This could also have a knock-on effect of disrupting the bowler's length and shift the power from the fielding side to the batting side.

HOW TO PLAY IT

This is a slightly premeditated shot insofar as you already need to have been planning to play it before the bowler lets go of the ball. However, when you are playing against spin, wait for the ball to be released from the hand before moving, otherwise you run the risk of a good spin bowler spotting you coming and adjusting their line and length.

Assess how the wicket is playing first. Is it fast, seaming or turning prodigiously? Be careful not to play it too early in your innings before you have assessed the situation fully.

There are three key elements to the movement down the wicket: the click; the crow-hop; the lead-in with the back foot.

It is very important that you go at the line of the ball with your head balanced and eyes level throughout. You don't want to have to lunge towards the ball at the last minute.

Look to strike the ball working your hands through the line, maintaining a strong base position throughout.

1. Click

2. Crow hop

3. Lead in with back foot

4. Work your hands through the line

TROUBLESHOOTING

- Take care if the ball is swinging, seaming around or spinning a lot.

- Don't move too early – it gives the bowler more chance to change the line and length.

- Don't lean back on the shot.

- Make sure your hands are following through the line of the ball.

- You can hit against the spin as long as you get on top of the bounce.

- Be prepared to adjust and just defend, or to manipulate the ball into a gap (see page 18).

- The rhythm and timing of footwork is key, so practise the shot regularly.

HOW TO PRACTISE IT

Beginner level
The first thing you need to do is learn the three key elements of the movement: the click, the crow-hop, the lead-in with the back foot. Getting the movements right is key to playing this shot. Practise this without a ball until you get it right and it comes naturally. Once this has been mastered, the coach can give tennis-ball drop-feeds ahead of the batter so they have to use their feet to meet the ball.

The shot can be struck along the ground, but more usually in the air. Concentrate on watching the ball and striking it as cleanly as possible.

Intermediate level
Here the coach can use bobble feeds – still with a tennis ball. The feed should vary with differing lines and lengths of delivery to force changes to the footwork – for example, the first stride may have to be bigger to meet the ball. Batters should aim to meet the ball on the second bounce. You can then move on to underarm one-bounce feed. Decision-making can be introduced by using different coloured balls to hit towards certain targets.

Advanced level
At the higher level, coaches can deliver rapid-fire drop feeds, six balls at a time. Batters move in a straight line with the coach moving forward with each drop feed, varying line and length. This can be progressed to a hard ball either with throw-downs or a bowling machine. A quick feed can be used for pace bowling, or slow speed for spin.

Batters shouldn't always look to strike big. Look to manipulate the ball – see page 18 – working ones and twos. As a further progression, the coach can call target areas as the ball is fed.

Fielding captain's note

Look to see if there are any pre-release cues that the batter is planning to use his feet. Ask your wicketkeeper if they've spotted anything that could help.

The keeper standing up to the stumps for the quicker bowlers can make batters think twice about using their feet, even if they are confident and proficient enough to do so (see page 108).

Bowlers can also vary the pace and/or length to disrupt the batter (see pages 59–66).

3. LOW FULL TOSS / YORKER-LENGTH STRIKING

Hitting a very full ball is difficult, but in Twenty20 cricket you are going to receive a lot of yorker-length balls – as well as failed near-yorker-length balls which don't come off, meaning low full tosses will inevitably come your way. Batters want to minimise the number of dot balls they receive, so need to find a shot to turn these balls into runs.

Essentially you are looking to turn a very full ball into a run-scoring opportunity by driving the ball on the half-volley or full toss.

HOW TO PLAY IT
Utilise the depth of the crease to adjust the length of the ball to suit you.

Playing the shot

Note the weight on the back leg

You can premeditate this shot: either by *starting* deeper in your crease in your stance, particularly if the bowler is already looking to bowl a full length; or by reading the length of the delivery *then* stepping back deeper into the crease. Either way, you'll need to create a strong base with a still head position centred down the middle of your body but slightly forward, weight on your back leg.

Free your hands so they can be explosive through the ball, either on the half-volley or full toss. The shot could be hit into any area in front of the wicket from square on the off-side to a delivery outside offstump, opening the face slightly – or to mid-wicket for a leg-side delivery squirted out into the leg side.

A variation is to move inside or outside the line to change the direction of the hit, sending it along the ground or over the top of the field if you can get enough elevation on the ball.

HOW TO PRACTISE IT

Introductory level
Start in your normal stance position with strong base, weight on back leg, head forward. The coach should provide an underarm feed on full, with batters striking the ball from their base position.

Intermediate level
From a stance position step back into your crease to underarm and overarm feeds. These can be done with various types of balls from tennis to incrediball or hardball, according to the age and ability of the batter. Coaches should *aim* to feed to a yorker length, which will naturally result in a varied length between half-volleys and full tosses through the margin for error.

Advanced level
Here a bowling machine is ideal to get a consistency of length. Hard-ball throw-downs can also work if the feed is good. Rapid-fire feeds add an element of playing under pressure.

TROUBLESHOOTING

- Be prepared to dig out or block the ball if you turn it into a yorker!

- Consider using a shorter backlift if a bowler hits a yorker length consistently.

- Watch the ball closely on to the bat.

- Keep a still head position – a moving head could be the difference between four runs and out!

- Keep a good solid base.

> **Fielding captain's note**
>
> Slower balls are effective here as batters may spoon the ball up in the air.
> Ask your bowlers to practise perfecting the art of the yorker, adjusting for batters using the depth of the crease.

MANIPULATING THE BALL

In Twenty20 cricket it is critical to keep the scoreboard ticking over and to avoid dot balls. In the 2010 IPL tournament, an average 40 per cent of deliveries (2.4 balls per over) were dot balls – perhaps a surprisingly high amount. You won't be able to hit every ball but if you can *reduce* the amount of dot balls, those extra one or two runs could be the difference between winning or losing.

Losing early wickets in a Twenty20 innings does make life difficult whether setting or chasing a target, so this might be the ideal time to manipulate the ball around the field for a few balls to consolidate the innings and ensure you use your full quota of overs.

It's a shot that can be played against any type of bowler. It's ideal for the middle overs when lower-risk shots might be necessary if early wickets have been lost.

As well as pushing the ball into gaps for singles, you can also look to turn ones into twos by hitting the ball with the right amount of pace towards a boundary fielder.

Threes are surprisingly rare in Twenty20 cricket, so twos become even more important if you can't hit boundaries.

During the powerplay overs of an innings, although you will be wanting to hit big as often as possible, manipulating the ball into gaps and turning ones into twos is just as useful.

Make sure you assess what would be a good total according to the conditions, wicket, etc. There's no point in going out trying to blast fours and sixes if it's a 120 wicket with the ball moving both ways of the seam and swinging!

HOW TO DO IT

It is critical that you visualise the potential scoring areas in the field. Think about the type of delivery you need to receive in order to play shots into each of those areas.

Every batter should be able to picture where the fielders are with their eyes closed.

Any area of the field should be accessible with any range of shots. With quicker bowlers, you can manipulate the ball using its pace to areas behind square. With slower bowlers, you have to create more momentum and power on the ball.

Examples of the potential shots batters might use include:
- chip shots over the infield
- glances or deflections to third man or fine leg
- soft hands, drop and run shots

Working the ball leg-side

Using the pace of the ball off the face of the bat

The key point is that after contact with the ball, with the full face of the bat, extend your bat and hands in the direction of your target area. More advanced players can use the wrists to work the ball into different areas.

HOW TO PRACTISE IT

Introductory level
Start with a bobble feed on the front foot, targeting hitting a ball into coned areas on the on- and off-side of the wicket.

Intermediate level
Move on to a bounced feed, playing off the front foot and back foot.

You can use one-handed drills with the top hand working the ball into a target, then adding the bottom hand back in; then bottom hand only back-foot shots, adding top hand back in later. Continue this using coned target areas as targets are really important here.

For variation and progression introduce coloured balls and coloured cones to make batters process information as they play. For example, ask them to hit a coloured ball into the same coloured coned area.

Hoops and target areas for chip shots, like golf practice, can be used too.

Advanced level

Here throw-downs or bowling-machine drills work best. If possible set up a middle-match play scenario adding fielders in place of the cones. This also adds the tactical awareness of whether fielders are left- or right-handed, which can be the difference between turning a one into a two, or turning a one into a 'sorry' as your colleague passes you on the way back to the pavilion!

Working the ball off the face of the bat to the off-side

TROUBLESHOOTING

- Decision-making is critical here. Think about shot selection, balancing whether to hit big or find gaps according to the match situation. Making the right choice and reducing the number of match errors you make means practising hard.

- Assess the type of wicket. Certain shots may not be appropriate on certain wickets.

- Watch the ball closely on to the bat and work the hands through the line.

- Be careful you don't overhit the ball and there isn't a one or two there when you think there is. Make sure you judge the run correctly.

- Ensure your running between the wickets is as effective as it could be (see page 52).

Fielding captain's note

Make sure your fielders are tight on ones and twos. Boundary fielders may just be thinking they are there to stop the fours and sixes, but in Twenty20 cricket when every run really matters, getting to the ball quickly is important too. Are your best fielders in the key areas?

Make sure your bowlers are alert to the 'drop and run' shot as they may be best placed to follow through and attempt a run-out. This is a skill in itself and should be practised in net situations and middle practices.

Read a batter's strengths and preference to work out which scoring areas they are looking to hit. This helps you set your field and suggest where bowlers should be looking to bowl. Remember yorkers (see page 64) are hard to manipulate, as are bouncers!

PICK-UP SHOT

This frequently used shot in Twenty20 cricket is typically played to a delivery on the legs, although you can step inside the line to turn it into the right ball for the shot.

Ideally you are looking to hit the ball aerial over the infield – to score a boundary, four or six – but it can equally be played to get over the infield for a single (see page 18).

This is the perfect shot for balls drifting down the leg side, utilising the angle and the pace. An in-swing bowler, or those bowling wide of the crease, would be someone who you could look to target for this shot.

HOW TO PLAY IT

It can be played to a short-, good- or full-length ball, but in different ways.

To a good- or full-length ball you go into a front-foot position, with the front foot in line to just outside the line of the ball. It is important that your head position stays in line with your front foot, eyes level.

At the point of contact you want to present the full face of the bat, rotating your wrists utilising the pace of the ball.

Predominantly back-foot players may also look to play this as a back-foot shot, especially to a fuller ball right under the eyeline.

To a shorter-length ball, you can look to get a bit further inside the line to pick it up finer behind square of the wicket, perhaps over the top of a short fine leg inside the fielding circle.

Front-foot pick-up: note the head position and eyes focused on the ball

Pick-up on the back foot

HOW TO PRACTISE IT

Introductory level
Start with an overarm feed using a tennis ball or incrediball at pace (you need the pace to utilise it for the shot). Practise initially getting the body into the correct position. Vary length of feed as consistency of shot improves. You can play it as front foot or back foot, whichever feels most comfortable.

Intermediate level
Move on to cricket ball throw-downs. If a middle practice or – if you are indoors – an open-hall scenario is possible, then introduce target areas too.

Advanced level
Bowling-machine feed or actual bowlers are best at this level.

If actual bowlers are delivering the feed, practise using your position in the crease to play the shot. This will compensate for the less regular position of the feed. It is also an excellent practise for improvisation.

TROUBLESHOOTING

- Use the pace of the ball; don't try to hit it too hard as you shouldn't need to do this.

- Don't close the face of the bat with bottom hand too dominant or it could go straight up rather than up and over.

- Don't get too far outside the line with your head.

- Don't sink on to the back leg too much.

Fielding captain's note

Increase the batter's risk levels by asking your bowlers to bowl to a good line and not towards leg. Consider setting a stronger leg-side field (bearing in mind that you can have no more than five fielders on the leg side) for in-swing bowlers or those that bowl wide of the crease.

UPPERCUT

6.

This was a favourite of Australian wicketkeeper-batsman Adam Gilchrist – probably one of the most destructive batters the game has ever seen.

It is a shot played to a short ball within arm's length, where you are looking to hit over the infield into an area from directly over the keeper through to third man.

The big advantage of this shot is that you are hitting towards an area where there are unlikely to be any fielders, so as long as contact is good, the chances of losing your wicket are remote and the chances of a boundary are high! A win-win situation.

The point of contact: note the bat position and eyes focused on the ball

HOW TO PLAY IT

The shot is played from a base/stance position, watching the ball really closely on to the bat and looking to make contact just past your eyeline, with hands behind you at head height.

Set your hands as if you were going to play a cut shot, but instead of going hard at the ball, angle the bat face slightly upwards. Allow the ball either to run off the face of the bat or elevate it with a last-second flick, rising with the bounce on to the balls of your feet if necessary.

This can be played either over the infield or looking to hit the ball for six behind the keeper!

With balls very straight aimed at the head, arch your back to give you a body position to be able to play the ball over the keeper/slip positions.

Note the back slightly arched here, as the ball is closer to the stump line

HOW TO PRACTISE IT

Introductory level
Start with high hands just behind your eyeline, ready for the shot, like you might do for giving slip practice. Tennis-ball underarm full-toss feeds at pace are best, with the natural variation of line that comes from human feeds.

Intermediate level
Move on to bounce feed with tennis balls, this time with the player in the stance position so they have to move into the ball. Increase to a rapid-fire feed as consistency of shot increases.

Advanced level
Hard-ball throw-downs or bowling machines, or ask your fast bowlers to pitch it short. Be prepared to duck out of the way and make sure you're wearing your helmet!

TROUBLESHOOTING

- Be careful of the ball that follows you! Have a plan for all eventualities.

- Don't turn your head – keep your eye on the ball. If you're turning your head on the ball this isn't the shot for you yet.

- Practise hard. You're hitting a small area of the bat at pace. It's not as easy as it looks.

- Caught behind is a big risk, so make sure you are getting sufficient elevation on the shot.

Fielding captain's note

Shorter balls are best bowled at throat level with no width. Width is a weakness in Twenty20 cricket so if your bowlers are going to bowl fast bouncers, make sure their direction is good – or look at using slow bouncers.

Sweep shots

The sweep shot has been adapted over the last few years to encompass many different variations, particularly since the advent of Twenty20 cricket.

Until the late 1980s, it was rare to see anything other than the traditional sweep shot to leg. Many will remember the infamous Mike Gatting **reverse sweep** of the 1987 World Cup final, leading to his downfall against the first ball from the part-time bowling of Australian captain Allan Border – a shot which probably cost England the World Cup that year. Gatting was far from the first who played the shot but he certainly brought the shot to the fore, if not sadly to the four!

More recently we've witnessed the sight of Marcus Trescothick **slog sweeping** the spinners for six at will – a shot that became his trademark.

Nowadays batsmen like Eoin Morgan and Kevin Pietersen use these shots as standard weapons for one-day cricket.

We'll take a look at both of these shots – along with the **paddle sweep** – and show you how to play them, and when.

Eoin Morgan plays one of his trademark reverse sweeps. Note the strong base and head position

SLOG SWEEP

7.

Whereas a traditional sweep shot will typically go square or slightly behind square of the wicket for anything up to four runs, the slog sweep is aimed at a different area – from just in front of square to cow corner – and is more likely to be a boundary-hitting shot. As we know, the ability to hit fours and sixes is a crucial skill in Twenty20 cricket, making this an important shot to master.

It is appropriate to play this throughout the innings, but it's important that you consider the pace of the wicket. You may not want to play this shot so readily on a slower wicket with little or inconsistent bounce, as you will struggle to get under the ball to elevate it over the infield (and hopefully the boundary).

Traditionally this shot would have been played against slow bowlers, but more recently players have been using it against medium-pace. Mal Loye

Mal Loye sweeps Brett Lee of Australia

catapulted himself into the England team largely because of his ability to innovate in limited-overs cricket; he used the slog sweep against express-pace bowlers at the start of an innings, forcing them to adjust their lines, lengths and field placings. A slog swept six off Brett Lee, then one of the world's fastest bowlers, on his debut – which certainly set the tone!

You will see wicketkeepers coming up to the stumps more often to medium-pacers these days to make it more difficult for batters to use their feet freely (see page 108).

HOW TO PLAY IT

You are looking for a length delivery and to hit the ball in line with your head.

This may mean that you could come across your stumps and play a slog sweep to a ball that would have been a distance outside off-stump, although it is clearly easier to play to a ball on the stumps.

As opposed to a traditional sweep shot where you put your front foot towards the ball, with a slog sweep you open up your front leg to be able to free your hands through the ball.

As with the traditional sweep shot, you collapse on to your back leg, but instead of hitting high to low, you are looking to hit low to high to get the ball over the infield and to the boundary. The bat face completes through the ball towards your target area, with your head remaining in a still and balanced position.

HOW TO PRACTISE IT

Beginner level
Start from the collapsed position with the hands at the top of the backswing. The coach should supply drop feeds then bobble feeds.

Intermediate level
Tennis-ball bobble feed from normal stance, dropping into slog-sweep position, opening up front leg. The coach should use coloured balls indicating where you want the ball to be hit.

Advanced level
Use hard-ball throw-downs and/or bowling machine. Look to call areas to hit the ball. From a collapse position and stance position.

Picking the length of delivery, eyes focused on the ball

Front foot opens up, stepping towards the ball. Note head in line with ball

Still head position and eyes focused on the ball at contact

Completion of shot with body-weight remaining forward

TROUBLESHOOTING

- Make sure the front leg is cleared out of the way. You don't want to be hitting your pads.

- Don't overhit the ball – timing is the key.

- Don't lean back on the shot. You need carry to get it over the boundary, and leaning back is more likely to send the ball straight up in the air.

- Don't choose the wrong ball. Once you're in that position it's difficult to adjust.

- Look for gaps in the field to increase your margin for error. You don't want to be hitting straight down a boundary fielder's throat if you can avoid it.

- Watch the ball carefully for changes of pace – you may have to adjust your timing.

> **Fielding captain's note**
>
> For batters who are looking to slog sweep quicker bowlers regularly, ask your keeper to stand up to the stumps if they can. Then batters have to consider the risk of a stumping when weighing up whether to play the shot.
>
> Get your bowlers to bowl more of an off-stump line or just short of a length to restrict the shot. However if the batter has a number of strong shots in their armoury make sure you are not adjusting to offer up an easier shot.

PADDLE SWEEP

8.

The paddle sweep is a more subtle sweep shot, hitting gaps in the field using the pace of the ball.

Often in Twenty20 cricket, due to the field restrictions at various times of the game, fine leg will be up in the ring or fairly square. With the paddle sweep you are looking to guide it very fine, almost just past the keeper, to a fuller-length ball. You should aim to utilise the pace of the delivery.

The paddle sweep is a 'touch' shot. It can be played to a slower bowler or indeed a medium-pacer.

First you need to assess the pace of the wicket. This is not necessarily a shot you are going to get full value from on a slower track, unless it is played to a full toss, as it may come on to the bat too slowly. With a slower delivery you might need to work the ball a little more, to ensure there is enough pace to get the ball down to the boundary.

It is feasible to play this shot to any ball pitching in line with the stumps, but the further towards off-stump it is, the more chance you are going to hit it onto the stumps or not fine enough.

HOW TO PLAY IT

Batters should prepare to play this shot from the hand – meaning you should try to pick the line and length of the ball from the second the delivery is released.

Get your head in line, or just outside the line of the ball, and forward over the top of your front leg. Collapse low, forcing your hands out in front, to make contact with the ball just in front of your front leg, or just outside.

Moments before impact

There is a greater element of risk to taking the ball from off-stump or outside the off-stump line, but it is possible with practise.

The toe of your bat should be angled to the ground, allowing the ball to work off the face. On contact you have the opportunity to angle the face to dictate the line the ball will go in after contact, looking to find the gap.

HOW TO PRACTISE IT

Introductory level
Start from the collapsed position with your hands out in front of you.
The coach is around eight metres away, down on one knee, feeding underarm with a tennis ball fairly firmly. Practise hitting the ball.

Intermediate level
Introduce coned areas to work on angling the ball into gaps. The coach should vary the line and length of delivery to make the batter think more.

Advanced level
Introduce a hard-ball feed or bowling machine at this stage. Coloured balls can be used to hit the ball to different areas according to the colour of the ball.

TROUBLESHOOTING

- Watch out for lbws. You may be putting your pads right in front of the stumps to play this shot so make sure you make some contact.

- Watch the ball closely on to the bat to ensure good contact.

- Stay balanced – you don't want to be toppling over.

- Don't flick or rotate the wrists too early; let the ball do the work. It's a 'touch shot' not a strike.

- Keep your head in line with the ball. This will help you get better contact.

- Get into the collapsed position, don't stand too tall.

- Don't pick the wrong ball – ideally it needs to be a good-length ball. Prepare a get-out strategy in case you get it wrong.

Fielding captain's note

Look at the positioning of your fine leg. Can you get them finer or deeper? Could there be a more athletic fielder there? Ask your bowler to bowl more outside off-stump and maybe not so full, or vary the pace. See what other shots the batter can play – make them work for their runs, don't let them take the initiative.

REVERSE SWEEP

9.

With the reverse sweep you are looking to manipulate the ball and take advantage of an unguarded area – in other words, third man/backward point, which may well not be protected due to fielding restrictions. It also works well as an attempt to throw the bowler off line and give them something else to consider.

As a batter you are always looking to take the initiative away from the fielding team, and the reverse sweep can really make them think about their strategies.

As with the normal sweep shot it is played on length, but if you misread the length you can look to adjust and play the reverse paddle. As opposed to the normal sweep, a ball closer to off-stump is preferable but not essential. The key is waiting as late as possible and watching the ball closely.

HOW TO PLAY IT

As with regular sweep shots, you collapse on to the back leg but your bottom hand comes over your top hand and goes leg-side of the ball, opening the face of the bat, striking the ball in front of the eyeline and in front of the front leg.

You are looking to strike the ball keeping the bat face open through contact and not angled towards the pitch. Maintaining a strong balanced base position with a still head is critical.

The shot can be hit along the ground or in the air according to the field placings, but clearly along the ground is a lower-risk shot as you are unlikely to be hitting a reverse sweep for six (see 'switch hit', page 46).

It's also possible to play the shot as a variation, leading with your back leg instead. The bat and hands still do the same but you lead with the back leg into a front-foot position and your front foot into a back-leg position. Balance is even more important here.

It's a premeditated shot so if you happen to get into position too early and the ball is fuller than expected, utilise the pace of the ball with a reverse paddle shot instead, guiding the ball instead of striking it. In addition, if it's shorter you could come out of the collapsed position slightly and play a reverse pull-type shot, or a reverse paddle to utilise the pace and direct the ball into a gap. Having a 'get out' shot if you get into trouble is important – it helps you build up enough confidence to add this shot to your armoury.

Strong base with eyes focused ready to strike the ball

Point of contact: note how the bat face has not closed

HOW TO PRACTISE IT

Introductory level
Start from the collapsed position with your hands out in front of you and already switched – this works with front-leg and back-leg positions. The coach/feeder should be around eight metres away, down on one knee, feeding underarm fairly firmly using tennis balls.

Intermediate level
Here use a rapid-fire feed starting from the collapsed position, moving on to crossing over and dropping from a stance position with an underarm or bobble feed. Coned areas can be introduced to help the batter angle the ball into gaps, or different-coloured balls can suggest hitting into different areas.

Advanced level
Here a hard-ball feed or bowling machine can be used, as well as coloured-ball drills for added decision-making. Hit along the ground or over the top.

TROUBLESHOOTING

- Don't get into position too early and give the bowler time to adjust.

- This is a higher-risk shot so make sure you are confident to play it.

- Prepare to adjust if it's the wrong ball. Practise your get-out shots to prepare for all eventualities.

> **Fielding captain's note**
>
> Think about field placement to a batter strong at playing the shot. Is your third man fine enough? Up in the ring? Ask your bowlers to adjust their line, length and pace to make it more difficult.

Unorthodox shots

The advent of Twenty20 cricket has meant that batters are increasingly finding different ways of making the fielding team work harder, and of hitting the ball into unguarded areas.

For example, the **switch hit** was popularised recently by Kevin Pietersen against the bowling of arguably the best spinner the world has ever seen: Muttiah Muralitharan. Pietersen probably wasn't the first to use this shot but it's certainly associated with him now. Even more recently, England's Eoin Morgan has been associated with the paddywhack, an alternative version of the same shot.

Similarly the **Dilscoop** was perfected by Sri Lankan batsman Tillekeratne Dilshan in the ICC World Twenty20 of 2009. Dilshan actually wasn't the first to play this shot. A very similar version is known as the Marillier shot after little-known Zimbabwean Doug Marillier, who first used it against Australian great, Glenn McGrath. New Zealand wicketkeeper-batsman, Brendon McCullum, is also a recognised exponent.

We will show you how to play both but they are not for the faint-hearted!

The game will continue to evolve, so always try to be creative in your batting.

DILSCOOP

10.

The Dilscoop (or lap shot) is a fairly new innovation. The earliest-known version, the Marillier shot, was first played at the turn of the 21st century.

It is a very high-risk shot and needs to be well practised before you attempt to use it in a match.

It is a touch shot, looking to target the gap in the field behind the wicketkeeper – an area which is always going to be unprotected.

As a batter you should be looking to play traditional cricket shots first, but there may be a time in the game where you need to try something different – for example, if you are falling behind the run-rate and you need to wrest the initiative away from the fielding team. If you practise hard enough and perfect it, you can use it in a match to turn a game!

HOW TO PLAY IT

In your mind you need to be looking to play the shot, but without committing to it too early. You need to come forward to a ball from just short of a length, to a

Tillekeratne Dilshan plays his trademark Dilscoop

Watch the ball on to the bat face

good-length delivery from a medium-pace to quicker bowler, so you can utilise the pace of the ball.

Come forward with your front foot and head in line with the ball. As with a paddle sweep, your hands should be out in front with the bat facing upwards.

Collapse (not necessarily fully) on to your back leg – the lower you get the better. You need to be brave and watch the ball as close as possible on to the bat face. Contact with the ball should be out in front and, as the ball hits the bat face, exploit the pace of the delivery and tilt the bat back towards the wicketkeeper. You should be aiming to hit the ball anywhere from over the keeper's head to fine leg.

You can either keep your head in line behind the bat or lean inside the line and look to manoeuvre the ball into the vacant area behind the wicket.

Don't try this without a helmet unless you enjoy counting teeth!

HOW TO PRACTISE IT

Introductory level
Start from the collapsed position. The coach should feed underarm tennis balls at pace, feeding wide of leg stump, with the batsman initially keeping the head outside the line to reduce the risk of hitting it directly into the face. Wear a helmet even if it's just tennis balls!

Intermediate level
Progress to a bounce feed – still with a tennis ball and still at pace. Feeds can be directed straighter and with more pace.

Advanced level
Progress to bowling-machine delivery with hardball. Work on a get-out shot to play if it turns out not to be the right delivery.

TROUBLESHOOTING

- Pick the right length of ball.

- Assess the surface you're playing on – consistent bounce is important to reduce the risk element.

- Pick bowlers with enough pace.

- Watch the ball as long as possible on to the bat; if you close your eyes or look away too early you could get into trouble.

- Your head must remain still to get the full effect.

- Stay low to get under the ball and work it over the keeper.

- Be aware of the position of fine leg. Up in the circle or back? If fine leg is back, this may not be the right shot.

- Practise hard to build confidence and reduce fear.

> **Fielding captain's note**
>
> Ask your bowlers to vary the line and length of the delivery. Look at the positioning of your fine leg – can you afford for them to be on the boundary?

FRONT-ON SQUAT LAP SHOT

11.

This shot is a very new innovation to Twenty20 cricket and executed by the likes of England's Eoin Morgan and Ben Scott of Middlesex. The key elements of this shot are total self-belief and backing yourself with bravery and flair. A totally premeditated shot, an element of luck is required for the ball to arrive in the ideal full- or yorker-length area, although the shot can still be adapted based on a shorter length. As with the Dilscoop it is a high-risk shot that needs to be practised regularly to master the skill.

HOW TO PLAY IT

The shot is played to the quicker bowlers – including the outright pace bowlers – as you need to utilise the pace of the ball. On release of the ball from the bowler's hand, the batter steps quickly into a front-on low squatting position with feet parallel to the batting crease and facing the bowler. The bat face is

Ben Scott gets into a perfect position to execute the shot

outstretched upwards and angled towards the ground with a slight bottom-hand grip-change moving underneath the handle, to allow the manoeuvring of the ball with a slight rotation of the wrist.

The ideal delivery for this shot is a yorker-length ball – allow the ball to work off the bat face, targeting either the off or on side behind square of the wicket, dependent on the line of the ball. If the ball is shorter in length, the batter will need to adapt by standing taller to keep the ball close to the eye line. Confidence is vital throughout the execution of the shot as you need to ensure the head does not move, duck or sway out of the way.

Note front-on position of the body

HOW TO PRACTISE IT

Introductory level
Start with the batter in a front-on squatting position. The coach underarms full toss or yorker-length feeds, varying the line. Allow the batter to get the feel of the required position, working the ball off the face of the bat.

Intermediate level
Start from a normal stance position. The coach increases the pace of a tennis-ball feed with overarm throws. Continue to vary the line of the feed and introduce different coloured balls to target hitting behind the off and on side. Additionally include shorter-length feeds to get used to balls that do not arrive on the ideal length.

Advanced level
Progress to hardball throw-downs and bowling-machine feeds, varying the line and length as mentioned above. Also build the shot into a net session utilising the shot against normal bowled deliveries.

TROUBLESHOOTING

- Wear a helmet at all times when practising the shot.

- Keep your head still and focus on the ball, watching it closely on to the bat throughout the shot.

- Make sure you are in a low squatting position.

- Practise hard and you will build confidence and reduce fear.

- Be aware of the fielders positioned at fine leg and third man, as the aim will be to manoeuvre the ball to the boundary finer of these positions.

> **Fielding captain's note**
>
> If the batter pulls this one off you can only really applaud the skill-level required; however if it is executed well consistently, the bowler must consider the change of length. The slower ball is also an option for the bowler although a skilled batter, if watching the ball really closely, can adapt. The captain must think about the positioning of fine leg and third man.

SWITCH HIT   12.

The switch hit effectively changes a right-handed batter into a left-hander, or vice versa. Usually this is achieved by reversing your hands on the handle, but not exclusively.

It became a controversial new addition to the batter's repertoire when Kevin Pietersen first used it. The game's law-makers were asked to determine the interpretation of the lbw rule as the batter's leg stump now effectively became off-stump and vice versa – but no changes were made.

It's a high-risk shot as it has to be premeditated and looks to target a less-well-packed field on the off-side, where fielders are more likely to be inside the fielding circle than patrolling all sides of the boundary. You need strong forearms to play this shot well, so it may not be appropriate for young or slight batters.

It is a shot which is most likely to be played towards the tail-end of an innings when you are trying to make things happen. You need immense confidence in the execution, and there is no substitute for practice here!

The shot may suit certain players more than others; perhaps people with a background in other sports – for example hockey, squash or hurling – where strong forearms are needed, or players with ambidexterity.

Most effective against slower bowlers, the batsman probably won't want to play it to anyone above medium-pace. The more confident you get, the quicker the bowler you can attempt it against, but it's not a shot to play to an out-and-out quick bowler.

HOW TO PLAY IT

In one movement, the batter switches their feet round to effectively take the stance of an opposite-handed batter (left or right), at the same time changing the hands round on the grip and landing in a strong base position.

Ideally you would be looking to hit a solid-base strike over what has now become mid-wicket (and which *was* cover/extra cover) from any length delivery. It doesn't matter too much when you change round in the bowler's run-up so long as you are in position with a solid base at the time of delivery. However the later you leave it the better, as it gives the bowler less time to adjust.

Playing the shot, step by step:

Step 1 *Step 2* *Step 3*

Step 4 *Step 5*

HOW TO PRACTISE IT

Introductory level

Practise strong-base striking (see page 8) opposite-handed: so play left-handed if you are right-handed and vice versa. Maintain a good solid base and a still head. Coaches should drop/bobble feed, then advance to throw-downs when the batter is becoming more confident and is striking the ball consistently.

Intermediate level
Here the batter should start from a normal stance, the correct way round. Turn hands and feet round on the coach's bobble feed, with the coach slightly increasing the pace of delivery when the batter's consistency of striking improves.

Advanced level
Once you have mastered the movement and are hitting the ball consistently, move on to hard-ball throw-downs, normal bowling or bowling-machine deliveries. The coach can suggest hitting target areas, and batters can look to use a flick of the wrist to send the ball into different areas of the outfield.

TROUBLESHOOTING

- Be prepared to play a different shot, particularly if the ball is outside of what is now off-stump – remember it's premeditated so the ball may not be there!

- Be flexible, adapting to the line and length of the ball as to where you play your shot.

- Maintain focus on the ball throughout the shot – there is a lot of movement involved and technically a lot can go wrong.

> **Fielding captain's note**
>
> There's not much you can do about this one! If a batter plays it and it comes off you've just got to sit back and applaud. Given the high-risk element of the shot, it's not something you should be too worried about as a captain. They're probably not going to play it more than once or possibly twice in an innings due to its high-risk nature, so maybe encourage the batter to play it more and hope to get a wicket!

FRONT-FOOT PULL / HOOK

13.

The traditional method of a pull or hook shot played to balls above waist- and chest-height is for the initial movement to go back and across, the aim being to get just inside the line of the ball.

With many batters initially intending to get on to the front foot to power-hit the ball in the Twenty20 format, we have seen a more frequent use of the pull and hook off the front foot to counteract the short ball in an aggressive fashion.

Ricky Ponting is a great example of how to execute the shot in all formats of the game.

Ricky Ponting demonstrates a perfect pull shot

HOW TO PLAY IT

The shot is played from the stance or forward-press position with your balance and weight pushing forward on to the front foot. From here, with quick decision-making to commit to playing the shot being vital, it is very instinctive. Your head must remain still with eyes focused on the ball throughout contact. Your arms should either be slightly flexed or extended somewhat straight, depending on the pace of the delivery, while you should rotate the shoulders horizontally.

The area you should aim to hit the ball into is dependent on the line of the delivery. The ball can be hit along the ground or in the air (which is more likely with the shorter-length delivery).

In a 2010 Champions Trophy Twenty20 match, Kieron Pollard hit a Shaun Tait 90mph delivery for a 120-metre six over wide mid-wicket using the front-foot hook!

HOW TO PRACTISE IT

Introductory level
With the batter set in a stance position wearing a helmet for protection, underarm feed tennis balls from 8–10 metres away, getting the batter to strike the ball cleanly while maintaining a still head and strong base.

Intermediate level
Move on to a bounce feed with both tennis and incrediballs while increasing the pace of the feeds. Additionally coloured tennis balls can be used to practise decision-making – perhaps requiring the batter hits the ball down or in the air, in front or behind square. Look to get the batter's momentum moving forward into a half-step position to play the shot.

Advanced level
Using a hardball, groove the shot further with a rapid-fire feed of six balls at a time with the batter's weight pushed on to the front foot and the head still. Repeat this process a few times to get into a rhythm. Move on to overarm feeds and bowling machine, increasing the pace of the feed and varying the length.

Point of contact: strong base and still head

The follow through

TROUBLESHOOTING

- Assess the pace and bounce of the wicket in case it's uneven.

- Watch the ball closely and do not follow the ball too early, although your momentum can take you into a swivel motion on the front foot.

- The back leg must remain strong to maintain and allow a solid striking position.

- Be brave and back yourself even though you may take a blow.

- It's a relatively high-risk shot: a bowler will be looking to induce a false shot so be prepared to pull out of the shot, particularly to a ball that bounces too high.

- Do not look to overhit the ball.

- Look out for the slower bouncer.

> **Fielding captain's note**
>
> In the powerplay overs the short ball is not necessarily a good option, with only two fielders outside the ring – particularly to a strong player of the short ball. Slow bouncers are a very effective delivery in Twenty20 cricket so discuss the option with your bowler during the innings.

14.

RUNNING BETWEEN THE WICKETS

In part five, we discuss the ways of training a cricketing athlete to work towards supreme physical conditioning. Meanwhile, the statistics suggest that a batter will predominantly run a high majority of singles, with far fewer twos, and threes only a rarity. We should therefore aim to improve in running between the wickets – this is a skill and needs training for independently of our batting technique, and in a manner specific to the Twenty20 format.

As in all formats of the game, decision-making, trust and communication between batting partners is crucial, but we should also consider some technical elements. Whether you're on strike or the backing-up non-striker, aim to get into a low, powerful running position as soon as possible when setting off.

The bat should be held with one hand near the end of the handle and the other holding the end of the bat to encourage a running-type motion with the arms. Once committed fully to the call, run in a straight line focusing on the other end only rather than watching the ball.

For a run single or return two, again get into a low position, and run your extended arm and bat in a metre or so before the line. Look to steal and scamper for every possible run without being too reckless.

The dive is a method that covers a lot of ground quickly; you need to be prepared to use this and it should be practised.

Half-turn position

Sprinter's turn position

The batter dives outstretched to make his ground

When touching and turning, it is crucial to get into a low position – this extends the distance covered – while watching the ball to see if a second run is viable. There are two positions the feet can set into at the turn: a half-turn and a sprinter's turn. Practise both to see which works best for you.

Additionally the non-bat-holding hand can support the body position at the turn by resting on the ground.

HOW TO PRACTISE IT

Introductory level
Simply get batters to shadow a shot, sprinting through the length of a pitch. Repeat the process and look for possible areas of improvement between each set. Move on to the turning technique, literally running in and out of a line from a 10-metre distance – make sure both left- and right-hand turns are used.

Intermediate level
With a tennis-ball feed, get the batter playing a shot on both the front and back foot. Allow them to get the feel of driving momentum into a sprinted run off the front and back leg (each is different). Additionally, introduce the outstretched dive, making sure they get low and parallel with the ground.

Practise running twos over the full length of the pitch, utilising the half-turn and sprinter's turn to see which one works best. A drill with a feed to a fielder on a coach call can also be introduced to create pressure for the batters.

Advanced level

Introduce a match-play scenario with a ring field set and batters under the instruction to work ones and twos working specifically on running, turning and communication skills as above.

TROUBLESHOOTING

- Practise your turns on the left- and right-hand side as one will be stronger. Some professionals will turn blind to the ball knowing that they are confident of making the two, particularly if they decide to turn on the quicker side.

- Call loudly, continuing to communicate while running and use eye contact to build understanding.

- Stay alert for overthrows.

- Run on a different line to your partner and make sure you don't collide with the bowler in the follow-through.

- When practising the dive use mats or powder indoors, and wet a surface outdoors – however be prepared to get dirty and graze a few elbows!

Fielding captain's note

Good running between the wickets can cause a well-drilled fielding team to fall apart quickly when put under pressure. It's important to remain calm, and to encourage and back your fielders. It's also useful to remember that one bit of great fielding can turn the momentum back in your favour.

PART TWO

BOWLING

INTRODUCTION

When Twenty20 cricket was first created by the England and Wales Cricket Board in 2003, the first year of domestic Twenty20 cricket in England was much more heavily skewed towards the batter than it is nowadays. Since then there have been a number of changes, but perhaps the biggest – an improvement in the athleticism of fielders apart – is the quality and creativity demonstrated by the bowlers.

Initially bowlers tended to run up and bowl in the same way they would have done in 45- or 50-over cricket, as it was played then; they soon worked out though that when a batting team has half the amount of available time, the innings plays out in a very different way, with expansive shots from the off.

It's ever more important in Twenty20s that bowlers work in partnership. The first and last balls of an over are inevitably the most important, as this is where the pressure is exerted or released. If the first ball of an over is a dot ball, the pressure is instantly on the batter. If it hits the boundary, the batter is immediately in the ascendancy and has the option of manipulating the ball for the remainder of the over, or of turning the screws by going for more boundary shots.

Similarly at the end of the over, a boundary can release the pressure on the batting team and put them in a stronger position for the start of the next over. A dot ball on the other hand will once again make the batter feel more pressure at the start.

The types of bowlers that are effective in Twenty20 cricket are different too…

In the first three years of IPL cricket (2008-10), of the top 15 bowlers with the lowest economy rate, ten were spinners and three (Lasith Malinga, Dale Steyn and Dirk Nannes) were

Lasith Malinga of Sri Lanka

out-and-out express-pace bowlers. Only two were medium or fast-medium bowlers. All 15 have an economy rate of between 6.4-7.4 runs per over.

Of the top eleven wicket takers seven are spinners, and over half also appear in the top fifteen low-economy-rate bowlers.

GAME PLAN

With bowling in Twenty20 cricket, strategy is very important. Are you looking to take wickets in the early overs to slow down the run-rate, or do you want to keep things tight? Questions like these should be addressed before the game.

Twenty20 cricket differs from the 40- or 50-over game in many ways, but one of the key things from a bowler's perspective is that the batter no longer has to guard their wicket as preciously in this format of the game, and so every bowler is treated the same – they're there to be hit! In that respect, on their day, a part-time bowler can end up being as effective as some of the world's most feared.

POWERPLAY BOWLING

The start of the innings is just about the only time when a bowler can get away with bowling anything approaching length deliveries. Early wickets in a Twenty20 match can sway the momentum hugely to the fielding side, so there is some sense in giving your opening bowlers licence to take wickets – possibly at the risk of going for a few more runs – in the hope of making the most of any early movement.

As soon as batters start to go after the bowling successfully and comfortably, it's time to think about a more defensive approach to the innings.

CHANGING PACE: SLOWER BALLS

15.

Slower balls have revolutionised limited-overs cricket, a format where batters used to dominate. In longer formats of the game, slower balls were used sporadically to provide a variation; nowadays it is not unusual to see an over of four, five or even six slower balls!

Typically aimed at the stumps (to limit the range of shots available to the batter), bowlers try for a good-to-yorker-length ball. However, the margin for error on a slower ball is that much less: if you get it wrong, it is a perfect six-hitting opportunity. They are hard to control initially, so practice is absolutely essential before it can become a dangerous weapon in your arsenal.

Slower balls work particularly well on slower pitches, and quicker bowlers have an added variation – the slower bouncer.

Ideally you want to keep batters guessing and use it as an element of surprise, but towards the end of an innings when batters are striking out a full over of well-controlled slower balls can be really difficult to get away for big runs.

Think twice about when to bowl them, though. If you are already on top, make sure it's the right time to bowl one. If you get it wrong and it sails over the boundary for six, could you lose the momentum in the game?

At the latter end of the innings when batters will be striking out even more, one option is to look to bowl wide of off-stump (being careful not to bowl a wide) as it upsets batters' timing as they look to fetch the ball to leg from outside off and it's significantly more difficult to hit without pace through the off-side.

HOW TO BOWL IT

There are several types of slower ball. Master one or two, you don't need them all.

Remember that disguise is the key. You don't want the batter to know you are bowling a slower ball until it's on them, so make sure they can't see if you've changed your grip and keep your arm speed the same.

Some different types of slower ball include:

1. Knuckle ball

With your middle finger bent behind the ball, grip the ball with your first and third fingers either side of the seam. Initially this will feel really strange and may be difficult if you have short fingers. Once you get it right, look for the extra swing that is often imparted, in addition to the ball coming out slower.

2. Back of hand

This ball is delivered with a leg-break hand action and can be done with or without implying spin. Without spin you can just grip the ball in your hand loosely and roll your wrist over at the point of delivery so the ball comes out in a loop. Alternatively you can grip the ball with a leg-spinner's grip and rip it out of the back of your hand; the seam rotates down the wicket and on most surfaces the ball should turn.

3. Wide grip

This delivery forces the ball out more slowly. Grip the ball as you would normally for a seam delivery, but place your fingers as wide as possible on the ball so it will still come out of your fingers. Be careful not to grip it too tightly or the ball will get stuck!

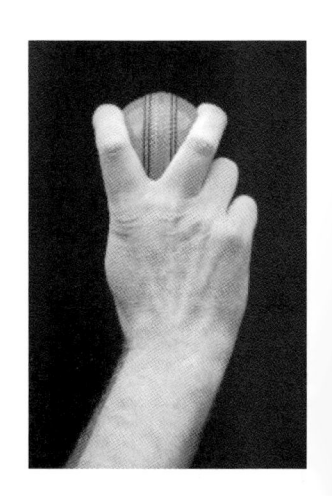

4. One-finger grip

A much harder to control delivery, this one. Grip the ball with thumb and forefinger only (down seam). Again, longer fingers will definitely help with control but it is possible for anyone to bowl this with practice.

5. Palm ball

Here the ball sits in the back of your hand rather than in the fingers. Don't grip it too tightly as you want the ball to float or be pushed out of your hand.

6. Cutter

An off- or leg-cutter can be bowled by rolling your fingers down the side of the ball – either side will work, depending on whether you are bowling off- or leg-cutters. The delivery won't necessarily be a vast amount slower but it will have the added bonus of movement off the pitch for the batter to contend with.

Leg-cutter

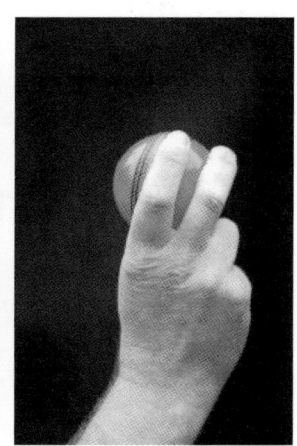

Off-cutter

7. 23-yarder

This delivery is bowled from roughly level with the umpire instead of by the front crease. Though it's often used by slower bowlers it can be used by any type of bowler. Fundamentally nothing much changes other than your release will be a bit earlier. Start your run-up from further back to accommodate it if you need to, but if you can bowl it without a change all the better, as you don't want to alert the batter. Be careful that you don't deliver the ball from behind the umpire as this is not allowed!

HOW TO PRACTISE IT

Robert Croft demonstrates the 23 yarder

Introductory level
Work in pairs, practising each different type until you find one or two that feel comfortable. Work on making it feel as natural as possible and delivering the ball with consistency of line and length.

Intermediate level
Once that has been mastered, move into the nets and work with target or coned areas. Look to hit the target as often as you can, concentrating on masking the grip and ensuring that your arm speed doesn't change noticeably.

Advanced level
You're ready now for a full practice environment with batters. Mix the slower balls in with normal deliveries. Does that batter pick them? If so, ask them how they spotted it, then go back and work on the deception.

TROUBLESHOOTING

- Bad slower balls are easy to put away, so make sure you practise hard to get it into the right areas to prevent them being picked by the batter.

- The margin for error is particularly small: ensure you are using them with confidence at the right time of the innings.

Fielding captain's note

Watch out for bowlers trying to bowl too many slower balls. Surprise is the key – unless they have mastered the art to a sufficient degree to get away with bowling them more often.

On the other hand if things aren't going your way and none of the bowlers have tried much variation, you might want to suggest slipping the odd slower ball in.

VARYING YOUR LENGTH: YORKERS

16.

The yorker is the ultimate weapon at the Twenty20 bowler's disposal.

It's probably the hardest delivery to master, but once you get it right it can be lethal, as has been shown by many experts over the years such as Waqar Younis and Darren Gough.

Aimed at the batter's feet in the 'block hole', you are targeting an area of only about 20cm either side of the popping crease. On the plus side, it does make it very hard to score runs off and could lead to a wicket.

You can bowl these at any time during a Twenty20 match but it's most often seen in the closing three or four overs. The best death bowlers will bowl a lot of yorkers. Alfonso Thomas of Somerset has become particularly adept at bowling death yorkers in English domestic Twenty20 cricket.

Clean bowled by a yorker!

Why not bowl them all the time? If you can deliver a consistent yorker length then that is obviously a bonus, but good batters will adapt and look to go back deeper in their crease to turn it into a half-volley length or move forward to turn it into a full toss. Overuse throughout the innings may not be all that useful, then.

HOW TO BOWL IT

With such a small target to aim for it is a difficult ball to master. Get it wrong and it's a low full toss or half-volley! But as ever, practice makes perfect.

At the top of the action you look to drive your shoulder through towards the target to get that extra fraction of length, and let go of the ball fractionally earlier.

In-swinging or reverse-swinging yorkers are particularly effective for exponents of swing, as demonstrated by Waqar Younis in the 1990s and more recently by another Pakistani bowler, Umar Gul.

In Twenty20 cricket, bowlers are now sometimes avoiding the more traditional leg-stump yorkers in favour of bowling wide of off-stump, as batters are finding ways of hitting leg-stump yorkers (see page 15).

HOW TO PRACTISE IT

Introductory level
Visualisation is the key to success with the yorker. Start with a basic coned target area and see how often you can hit it.

A raised target is an even better starting-point. Give yourself more of a chance to begin with and line up three or four targets in a row, like a shooting gallery at the fairground. See if you can knock them all down.

Intermediate level
Reduce the target area once you are hitting the target regularly to make it more challenging.

Advanced level
Close your eyes just as you deliver the ball and get the feeling of driving your momentum through the ball. Look to bowl in-swinging yorkers if you can, for that extra element of surprise and to make it more difficult for the batter to use their crease to adjust.

TROUBLESHOOTING

- Get it wrong and it's a low full toss or half-volley, so practise hard to reduce your margin of error.

- If you're consistently too full or too short, look at your release point – is it too early or too late?

- Don't drive your shoulder through too hard as it could throw you offline or too full.

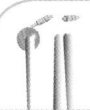

> **Fielding captain's note**
>
> For bowlers who are bowling consistently full, look to move fielders squarer or finer within the limitations of where you can have fielders. Batters will tend to be squirting out yorkers more often than they'll be driving through the covers or mid-wicket.
>
> Batters with higher skill levels will be going deeper into the crease or batting outside of their crease, so speak to your keeper about coming up to the stumps (see page 108).

17.
BOWLING CROSS-SEAM

Cross-seam bowling is far from new, but how it's been used has certainly changed. Bowlers used to hold the ball across the seam, especially with the white ball, when the ball was swinging excessively causing them to lose control and bowl wides.

More recently bowlers have used it as an attacking tool by using the inconsistency of bounce that comes with not knowing on which part of the ball it is going to land.

If it hits the seam on landing it might produce extra bounce or sideways movement. If it misses the seam, it will more likely kiss the surface and skid on quicker than anticipated.

The beauty of this is that as the bowler has no idea what is going to happen, the batter has no chance of working it out until it's too late!

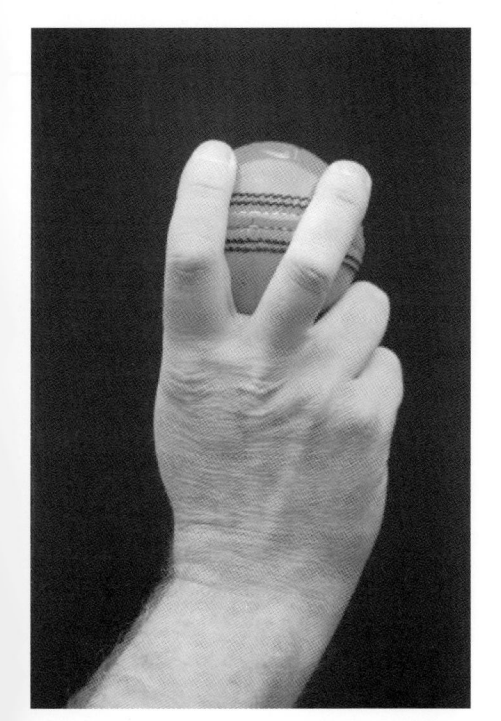

Cross-seam grip

HOW TO BOWL IT

There is very little difference between bowling a cross-seam ball to a normal-seam delivery other than the change of grip: the fingers go across the seam rather than either side.

HOW TO PRACTISE IT

Introductory level
In pairs, practise bowling the ball cross-seam. Concentrate on getting a consistency of line and length.

Intermediate level
Move into the nets and set up a target area. Look at what happens to the ball after bouncing – does it bounce more or less; does it skip on?

Advanced level

Bring in a batter and see how they adjust to cross-seam deliveries. Mix them up to introduce the element of surprise.

TROUBLESHOOTING

- Make sure the grip is comfortable. Holding the ball across the seam doesn't feel natural so it's important that it comes out of the hand correctly.

- Concentrate on consistency of line and length: you don't want a surprise ball to turn into a bad ball through poor execution.

> **Fielding captain's note**
>
> This is a great surprise delivery for your more accomplished bowlers to try if things are not going your way and you need to take a wicket to get the game back, so consider suggesting it.

18.
BOWLING AT THE DEATH

If the first few overs of a Twenty20 innings set the tone, the last few often decide the match. A good death bowler will need a number of different skills, but consistency of length and the ability to perform under pressure are perhaps the two most important.

Your best death bowler, usually those that are good at executing yorkers consistently, should bowl the eighteenth and twentieth overs of the innings.

Left-arm seamer Zaheer Khan has been a very effective death bowler in the IPL. Dale Steyn of South Africa is another master of the art.

Zaheer Khan (left) and Dale Steyn, both in action during the 2010 IPL

Batsman digs out Steyn delivery

HOW TO BOWL IT

At the end of an innings you need the correct mixture of yorkers, slower bouncers, slower balls and other changes of pace or angle of delivery coming round the wicket, according to which areas the batter is looking to hit.

Bowlers who bowl around the late 80mph to early 90mph are generally the most effective.

What you want to avoid is bowling a length delivery, as the batters will undoubtedly be looking to hit big runs. A delivery offering the batter width is similarly to be avoid, as it provides them with the opportunity to free their arms.

HOW TO PRACTISE IT

Introductory level

Set up target areas to avoid bowling length – concentrate on yorker and bouncer lengths especially. Use just one stump to focus your concentration. This is a good technique for all bowling practices.

Intermediate level

Bring a batter into a net and set a scenario – for example, 30 runs off four overs – to put the bowler under pressure to bowl in the key areas. Start off with the benefit of doubt on runs scored to the bowler, and gradually change the emphasis towards the batter to add extra pressure.

Practise with left- and right-handed batters to get used to adjusting your line – if you have one of each, use the two batters in the net running between the wickets every third ball so you have to adjust the line regularly. Practise bowling over and round the wicket to cramp the batter up.

Advanced level

Move on to a middle practice with two batters, fielders and scenarios. This is also a good practice for your batters, requiring them to strike big runs at the end of an innings.

TROUBLESHOOTING

- Don't bowl length!

- Don't bowl width!

- Keep your head together if you do get hit for runs. Coolness under pressure is essential for a death bowler.

- Don't bowl no-balls or wides. An extra ball, extra runs and possibly a free hit at this stage of the game could be the difference between winning or losing.

> **Fielding captain's note**
>
> Help take pressure off your bowler by getting the field right. Think about the areas the batters are trying to hit and protect them as best you can within the fielding restrictions.
>
> Support your bowler with encouragement if things don't go right. As captain you have to put your disappointment behind you to keep morale high.

BOWLING SPIN 19.

Spin bowlers have had a new lease of life in Twenty20 cricket, and it's not unusual for teams to field as many as three spinners in their starting XI instead of the usual one or two.

England won the ICC World Twenty20 in 2010 using two spinners – Graeme Swann and Michael Yardy – as one of their main weapons. Yardy is a fine example of the type of previously unfashionable slow bowler whose variation and 'darts' in Twenty20 cricket have been match-changing. Equally, although different, Swann gets massive revolutions on the ball with his big hands, causing a deceiving loop.

Pakistan's Saeed Ajmal and of course the great Muttiah Muralitharan have also been very effective attacking spin bowlers in Twenty20 cricket.

It is usually the big spinners of the ball who tend to do the best in the shortest form of the game.

Graeme Swann in action during the World Twenty20 2010

HOW TO BOWL IT

Bowling spin in Twenty20 cricket requires a good variation in your armoury. A combination of quicker balls, slower balls, subtle changes in flight, large amounts of spin, doosras, arm balls and googlies for leg spinners can all be really effective.

Spinners in Twenty20 cricket look to bowl quite full, as anything length will be easy to hit for big runs, and anything short can be worked or pulled away with ease unless it is turning greatly. Wide of the stumps is to be avoided too, as you don't want to give the batter width to free their arms.

Muttiah Muralitharan in action

HOW TO PRACTISE IT

Introductory level
Start by practising all the variations in pairs. Work together on the disguise element – how early can you spot what the bowler is delivering?

Intermediate level
Once the variations have been worked on, move into a net and set up target areas to ensure you can regularly hit the best lengths (yorker and very full) and also the best direction (straight). A raised target at the right length makes for excellent practice. Start with two or three in a row and remove them gradually as accuracy improves. This may take some time, but the more you practise the more accurate you will become.

Advanced level
Now you're ready for a batter. Watch how batters use their feet to come out to the ball, and use the crease to hit you into other areas (see page 12). Work hard on deceiving the batter and try to keep your eyes on them as long as possible – you want to try and catch their movements, creating a stumping opportunity by unexpectedly varying the line, pace or flight.

TROUBLESHOOTING

- Until you are used to it, bowling a lot of variation can easily throw you off line as a spinner as it's not so easy to get the right rhythm so work really hard and practise bowling six balls in a row with variation to replicate a match situation as closely as possible.

- Keep your control and flight. Spinners can easily bowl too flat when bowling quicker deliveries but you don't need to. Flight is one of the most important weapons a spinner has so don't lose it.

Don't let your head go down if the batters do go after your bowling. As a spinner many batters see you as the easiest option to target but you have the variations to be able to nullify the batter so don't panic – your time will come.

> ### Fielding captain's note
>
> Be prepared to start with spin – even at both ends – in Twenty20 cricket. Opening batters are not necessarily as comfortable at playing spin as lower-order players and they often prefer the pace of the ball coming on to the bat so early spin could give the innings a positive momentum. Plus you get through early overs quickly which puts pressure on your opponents. Make them feel hurried.
>
> If the spinners are bowling well and you haven't used up all of their overs early on, look to use them at times in the game when things are running away from you as they can be very effective in bringing the momentum back to you.
>
> As a general rule you should know your ideal bowling order in advance of the game. Who is going to open, for how long, who is first and second change, back-up and who is going to bowl at the death? Things don't always go to plan but it is important that you have a plan. Which end you open from could be important too. Is there a longer straight boundary at one end? If so, that might be the best end to bowl the twentieth over from to minimise boundary hits at the end of the innings.
>
> Be prepared to switch your bowlers around. Don't let the batter settle with one type of bowler for five or six overs as they will start to formulate a plan of attack. Try one-over spells to throw them off.

PART THREE

FIELDING

INTRODUCTION

One area of the game of cricket that has improved vastly over the past two decades is undoubtedly fielding.

The introduction of limited-overs cricket, and the need for players nowadays to be genuine athletes, has resulted in some amazing diving catches, slides to retrieve a ball and direct-hit run-outs from all areas of the pitch. These changes have since filtered down to all levels of the game.

Fielding innovations almost seem endless as Twenty20 cricket pushes cricketers' skill levels to an unimaginable standard at the top tier of the game. The format, with one or two runs either way impacting the result, has further highlighted the need for an all-round quality fielder.

In days gone by your less-competent fielders would be hidden out on the boundary. Now, however, you will see the best 'gun' fielders of the team sweeping either side of the wicket on the boundary, with specialist fielders at long-off and long-on.

Many coaches will highlight the importance of putting the same amount of time and effort into fielding as you would your batting and bowling. This is so important in Twenty20 where a batting team can run away with a game in a short space of time. As we have seen time and again, a great piece of dynamic, quick-thinking fielding can have a huge bearing on the result.

In this section we will cover many innovations, from a sliding stop and throw at the stumps to a flick-back catch from the boundary – all now common occurrences during a Twenty20 match. Fielding will continue to evolve and therefore we should be prepared to be creative and innovative in the way we think, train and coach fielding skills to produce attacking, smart-thinking and athletic fielders.

RETRIEVE / STOP AND DRAG BACK

20.

HOW TO EXECUTE IT

A good dynamic set position low to the ground will enable you to push off and turn in either direction to pursue the ball. The main objective is getting the ball back in the air as quick as possible and stopping the batter taking two runs, or creating a run-out situation (rarely do you see threes in Twenty20 cricket).

The timing of the drop and slide are vital to allow you to get close and next to the ball, according to the pace at which the ball is travelling.

On approaching the ball get low, dropping onto your non-throwing thigh; make sure you clear your collapsed knee and prevent your foot from digging into the turf and causing serious injury.

The non-throwing left arm (in the case of a right-handed thrower) will act as support as it plants on the ground while picking up the ball at the same time.

Note this left-handed fielder's use of the supporting arm

Your outstretched right leg and left hand will act as a brake, helping you to push up into a strong throwing position.

Additionally there are various modern adaptations of the slide where the ball is travelling towards the boundary line: the quickest method to stop the ball is to use the slide as above, flicking or dragging the ball back before it crosses the boundary line and making sure no part of the body is in contact with the rope while touching the ball.

HOW TO PRACTISE IT

Introductory level
Start in the finish position on the ground to get the feel of the required positioning of the body. Once comfortable with this, run slowly towards a stationary ball, making sure you get low on approach, looking to time your dropping movement to the ground to coincide with your throwing hand picking the ball up.

Intermediate level
The coach rolls the ball out slowly with the fielder pursuing the ball looking to get low into the slide. Once again the timing of the drop and slide are key, to coincide with the ball rolling into the hand. From this position pop up into a throwing position.

At this stage introduce a boundary line to practise the drag-back skill as discussed above.

Advanced level
Increase the speed, direction and length of feed to work the fielder hard. By this stage the fielder should be competent at the skill of dropping into the retrieve position at pace.

Look to introduce a batting pair running between the wickets to make it match-realistic, putting the fielder under pressure.

Make sure a strong throwing position is maintained with good alignment. When practising the drag-back skill, make sure the fielder gets up on to their feet quickly after crossing the boundary line for the return throw.

TROUBLESHOOTING

- Health and safety is of prime importance when this skill is practised as there is potential risk of injury (Simon Jones of England badly injured his cruciate knee ligament attempting the slide retrieve).

- If practised indoors make sure tracksuit bottoms are worn with mats and talcum powder an additional option to avoid friction (although be aware that powder can spread onto other areas of a hall making another potential hazard). If practised outside, especially in the case of younger cricketers, water an area that you are looking to practise in and be prepared to get dirty!

- Repetition and regular practise are the key elements to gain confidence in this skill.

- With young cricketers make sure the slide is practiced by players who have been coached correctly in the skill.

- Assess the area you intend to use for the practice.

> **Fielding captain's note**
>
> Encourage all members of the team to practise the skill and, when mastered, to bring it into match play. It can save many runs, produce potential run-outs and put doubt into a batter's mind.

21. STOP / FLICK-BACK SLIDE (HUNT IN PAIRS)

HOW TO EXECUTE IT

As with many aspects of modern fielding, you will often see one or two fielders support the actual fielder of the ball. They will run close to the main fielder and be in a position where the flick/drag back can be directed straight into their hands. As a result the ball gets into the hands of someone in a throwing position much faster, whether retrieved from within the outfield or close to the boundary line. This is a great method for saving runs and getting the ball back in for a potential run-out.

Hunting in pairs

HOW TO PRACTISE IT

The flick-back

Introductory level
In pairs, start with one fielder in the slide-retrieve finish position next to a stationary ball, with the second fielder four metres away already prepared in a throwing position, waiting to receive the ball. The ball is then flicked back directly into the hands of the thrower, who shadows a throw or throws to a third fielder.

Intermediate level
Still using a stationary ball, one of the pairs runs towards the ball from over a short distance looking to get low into a slide-retrieve position, flicking the ball back directly into the hands of the thrower, who releases the ball as above.

Advanced level
At this stage introduce stronger feeds at varying lengths and direction with the two fielders pursuing a moving ball-feed together. Also use a staggered start to allow more communication between the fielders on approaching the ball, as this is key. Additionally the two fielders can approach the ball from different starting-points or angles.

Match-play scenarios can be built into the practice with batters running between the wickets to create a pressure situation, and a keeper and fielder waiting in place for a return throw into the stumps.

TROUBLESHOOTING

- The health and safety issues are as per the slide/retrieve section (see page 78).

- Although your prime focus is the ball, awareness of the fielders supporting you is vital – develop peripheral vision and communication between fielders.

- Do not flick back just for the sake of it as it may well be quicker for the retrieving fielder to get the ball back in. This decision-making will come with practice and experience.

SLIDE INTERCEPTION

22.

HOW TO EXECUTE IT
The same method of slide is utilised as with the retrieve slide (see page 78), but the aim is to intercept a ball while fielding on the boundary or in the inner ring.

Open hands out in front of the eyeline

Both feet cleared from the surface

As the ball is hit into the outfield the fielder runs at pace, timing the slide to meet the ball as it rolls directly into the open hands. This allows the fielder to pop up quickly into a throwing position.

For a ball that is hit to the left the drop will be on the right side of the body, and for a ball hit to the right it will be on the left-hand side of the body. In most cases two hands can be used to pick the ball up underneath the eyeline.

This is also a useful method for the bowler to field off his own bowling, particularly when the ball is pushed for a single towards mid-on or mid-off and the fielders are back on the boundary either side of the wicket.

HOW TO PRACTISE IT

Introductory level
Start in the finish position on the ground to get the feel of the required positioning of the body. Once comfortable with this position, run slowly towards a stationary ball, making sure you get low on approach. Time your dropping movement to the ground to coincide with your hands cupped outwards meeting the ball. Practise landing on both your left- and right-hand side.

Intermediate level
The coach rolls the ball out slowly from 10–15 metres away to both the left- and right-hand side of a facing fielder who runs towards the ball looking to get into a low slide position. Once again the timing of the drop and slide are key to coincide with the ball rolling into the hands.

From here pop up into a throwing position. At this stage a boundary line can be introduced to the practice.

Advanced level
Now the coach can increase the speed and direction of the feed to stretch the fielder hard to both the left- and right-hand side.

With the higher level of competency at this stage, introduce a batting pair running between the wickets to make the practice realistic and to put the fielder under pressure.

On popping up into a throwing position make sure the fielder aligns feet, hips and shoulders to complete a strong throw, although this is not always possible in a run-out situation.

Additionally this skill can also be practised in pairs by flicking the ball outwards to an oncoming fielder if this is a quicker and better option.

TROUBLESHOOTING

- The health and safety issues are as per the slide/retrieve section.

- In most cases a fielder will have a stronger side to drop on to, so be prepared to practise the weaker side or use an alternative method if not comfortable.

ROLL-OVER INTERCEPTION

23.

HOW TO EXECUTE IT

This is a method used while fielding on the boundary, and when you want to intercept the ball while running parallel to the boundary line.

For a right-handed thrower, approach a ball hit to your right by dropping low into an almost long-barrier-type position with your left leg collapsed and your right foot behind the line of the ball. In one complete movement your momentum should take you into a 180-degree roll, leading with your right shoulder across your back. This will allow you to pop up into a strong throwing position.

Pick-up under eyeline

Roll onto throwing arm shoulder

From shoulder onto back

Momentum brings you back up onto your feet, helped by throwing arm

Align feet, hips and shoulder to throw the ball

The opposite can be achieved if approaching the ball hit to your left with the right leg collapsing and left foot behind the ball. Also this can of course be used for a left-arm thrower.

HOW TO PRACTISE IT

Introductory level
From a stationary long-barrier position, roll over your shoulder/back practising both left- and right-hand rolls with a ball in your hand. Look to pop back up into a throwing position making sure you are aligned with your target.

Intermediate level
The fielder approaches a stationary ball getting low to pick the ball up and using the momentum to completing the movement into the roll, popping up to release the ball. Practise both left and right feeds.

Advanced level
Here use feeds hit at pace from 20 metres to either side of the fielder introducing batters running between the wicket to create pressure and need to get the ball aerial quickly without compromising technique and potential injury.

TROUBLESHOOTING

- As with many aspects of fielding skills, look to get low early and be careful that the leading foot does not dig into the ground.

DIVING SLIDE

24.

HOW TO EXECUTE IT

The diving slide is used when you need to gain maximum distance at quick speed to either drag the ball back from the boundary or take it cleanly in the hand, popping up in one movement to release the ball from a kneeling or standing throwing position.

The key is to get low on approaching the ball, diving over a strong flexed leg on to your belly and thighs while initially clearing your arms and feet from the ground.

When executed in the inner ring, the front leg can be cleared and outstretched, allowing a strong throw directly at the stumps from a kneeling position. You can also pop up into a standing position if a stronger throw from the outfield is required.

Diving slide in action

Additionally with batters looking to elevate the ball in Twenty20 cricket the ball will also fall short of the boundary line. In this case a fielder will have to practise the skill of diving and stopping an aerial ball from just after the bounce.

This method is also used to take high catches that cannot be reached normally but are caught outstretched and low to the ground.

HOW TO PRACTISE IT

Introductory level
Over a short distance practise running into a dive-out over your strong leg, landing on your belly and thighs and making sure you get low to reduce any friction.

Intermediate level
With three stationary balls positioned in an arrow formation, the fielder initially walks out to a cone set in front and in line with the furthest middle ball. From this position the fielder practises the required hip-turn, diving out over a strong leg to the left- then right-hand-side balls, and additionally to the centre. The speed of the approach and distance of the balls can be increased as the skill level improves.

Advanced level
Introduce a moving ball, completing the dive with a throw over shorter and longer distances. To replicate the dive for fielding within the inner ring, place three or four stumps at different angles with the fielder practising throwing the stumps down from a kneeling stance, swivelling into a position to hit one of the stumps as directed by the coach.

To make the practice more realistic bring in batters to run between the wickets.

TROUBLESHOOTING

- Make sure relevant safety precautions are taken, either watering a surface outdoors or using mats/talcum powder indoors.

- Getting low is vital to take the impact.

- Creating a strong base on the throwing leg when throwing from a kneeling position.

25. ONE-HANDED PICK-UP AND SIDE-ARM THROW

Fielders at the top end of the game have become highly skilled at picking the ball up one-handed at pace, and in one movement releasing the ball with power from a side-arm position.

This is not necessarily a new innovation, as many West Indian cricketers have used the method over the years, although it is now very common in all formats of the game.

The main benefit of a side-arm throw is the speed at which the arm can be pulled back into a ready-to-throw position – unlike the further distance the arm and hand have to travel to get into an overarm-release position.

An overarm-release position may well produce more consistency of direction when throwing; however, with practice the side-arm release is quick and very effective.

Whether throwing side-arm, overarm or even underarm, fielders in the inner ring should be looking to hit the base of the stumps to reduce the margin of error. The logic being that if you miss the base, the ball will either bounce up and hit the stumps, or hit halfway up. If you aim for the top of the stumps, the throw could easily go over the top.

HOW TO EXECUTE IT

For a right-handed thrower, when the ball is hit to your right-hand side you will need to approach the ball in a low dynamic position, picking the ball up close to your non-throwing left foot.

In one movement the ball is picked up and with your arm extended but flexed back behind your body, almost parallel to the ground, the ball is released toward the stumps.

Although your momentum is working away from the target, power can also be gained from your right-hand side leg and hip, driving through off your left foot base.

Additionally you can look to throw the ball while off the ground, particularly if you are throwing at the stumps behind you, which will create more power in the throw.

Arm pulled back to throw

Elbow ahead of hand at release

Momentum takes thrower off the ground

If approaching the ball hit to your left, you will need to get around the ball to enable you to pick the ball up in your right hand. The quickest method of release is an open-body position, again making sure the arm is pulled back behind your body.

HOW TO PRACTISE IT

Introductory level
Initially walk through the process of picking up the ball to both your left- and right-hand side, to make sure the required footwork is correct. Release the ball with a side-arm throw.

Intermediate level
With the coach rolling balls out from a set of stumps, work the fielder between two cones left and right to practise the pick-up from both sides.

Do three or four feeds on each side, increasing the speed of feed as the skill-level improves.

Advanced level
Set up a drill with two batters running between the wicket. Roll a feed out to the fielder to their left and right within the inner ring. The aim is to get the ball back either to an additional fielder at the stumps, or hitting the stumps directly.

TROUBLESHOOTING

- Although the footwork remains the same, some fielders may prefer the overarm method so stick with what suits the individual.

- Coach or feeder to use mitt to prevent sore or bruised hands.

> **Fielding captain's note**
>
> Think about putting your quick and agile fielders in these positions within the inner circle. It will certainly put pressure on the batters and make them think twice about sneaking a single.

DIVING CATCHING

26.

HOW TO EXECUTE IT

While fielding in the inner ring you will automatically look to create good rhythm, walking in with the bowler on the balls of your feet then getting into a 'set' position as the ball is struck.

In the set position you should have a good posture with a flattish back, knees flexed to create a low base, feet slightly inwards and hands prepared out in front of your eyeline. It is personal preference whether the hands are close together or further apart.

From this position you can push forward with a strong hip-turn leading your head towards the ball – the aim is to get either one or two hands behind the ball, depending on the distance of the ball from the body.

Big open target (hand) as head goes to the line of the ball

The skill of landing on the ground is just as important as taking the catch: firstly you do not want the ball to pop out on impact; secondly you don't want to land badly and suffer a shoulder injury.

There are two approaches. Either the body can be in a front-on position to the ball at the point of catching, and turn to land on the chest/belly clearing the hands on impact, or alternatively before hitting the ground front-on, the body rotates onto the opposite shoulder, causing you to roll on to your back.

HOW TO PRACTISE IT

Outstretched diving catch: note the eyes focused on the ball

Introductory level
Start in a set position creating a low centre of gravity. Feed balls to both the left and right of the catcher, who should initially remain in a standing position to get the feel of their hips rotating and taking the head towards the ball.

Intermediate level
Push the feeds wider to both the left and right, getting the catcher into a

Create realistic edges in practice sessions

dive. Practise both the methods described above. As they become more proficient, ask the catcher to walk into a set position; then test them by further extending the height and length of feeds.

Advanced level

With the advent of modern coaching aids, consider the use of a Katchet, Crazy Catch or bowling machine to feed and test the catcher's skills to a higher level.

Additionally simple drills can be set up with overarm throws (bounced or full) in towards a batter who either strikes the ball with the full face of the bat, or edges it, thus demanding responses from different fielding positions.

Alternatively feed balls above the eyeline left and right, making the fielder jump off the ground. Try to create hang time to take the catch.

TROUBLESHOOTING

- Don't take your eye off the ball.

- Don't snatch at the ball.

- Diving is very physical so groove your body through lots of practice. If done incorrectly it can cause injury.

- Make sure you look to anticipate and read the line of the ball off the bat.

- Utilise mats and a wet surface where possible.

> **Fielding captain's note**
>
> As with many aspects of cricket, there are some fielders who will inevitably be stronger in certain areas. Therefore look to place your best diving catchers in the key positions for this skill, such as point and backward point. England's Paul Collingwood is a fine example of this skill.

27. DIVING FORWARD CATCH

HOW TO EXECUTE IT

When a ball is struck landing short of a fielder, diving forward to take a catch is a very difficult skill to master. The main problem is that you are throwing your momentum towards a ball that can potentially fly up into your face if the movement is mistimed.

The key is to back yourself, which will require a certain amount of bravery. From your dynamic set position as the ball is struck, you will need to dive forward into a lower position, leading with your head and keeping your arms outstretched.

Importantly the hands, or one hand, should be cupped upwards with the fingers outstretched. The aim is to create a scooping action under the ball while not taking your eyes off it.

Fielder takes catch diving forward

After wrapping your fingers around the ball you will naturally find that the momentum will take you into a rolling position on shoulder and back, using your stronger side.

If at any point you do not feel confident that you are going to make the catch, make sure you clear you head from the line of the ball.

HOW TO PRACTISE IT

Introductory level
Using tennis balls, position the fielder in a kneeling position and feed underarm throws out in front. The fielder should drop forward to take the catch. Vary the line of the feed.

Intermediate level
From a standing position, using tennis balls or incrediballs, underarm feed out in front, with the fielder diving forward to take the catch. Vary the line and speed of the feed.

Advanced level
Here the fielder walks into a set position with hard-ball feeds aimed out in front, pulling the catcher forward into a dive position to take the catch. Additionally the skill can be practised with high catches running forward into the dive.

TROUBLESHOOTING

- Make sure you dive low, getting parallel with the ground.
- Don't land on your elbows.
- Be careful practising with the hard ball.

CATCHING ON THE MOVE

28.

HOW TO EXECUTE IT

A ball that requires you to catch it on the move is more than likely to have been hit above the eyeline. This potentially should allow you enough time to reach the ball. It can be a catch that is taken coming forward to meet the ball, to the left or right, or over your shoulder.

The key elements are moving quickly to the area in which the ball might land, maintaining a still head with eyes focused on the ball throughout.

Speed, agility and hand-eye coordination are key skills that will enhance your execution of this catch.

Under normal circumstances you would coach a player to take the ball at or just above eye-level; however, this will not always be the situation – you are likely to have to take the ball with your arms outstretched in front or behind you, at varying distances from the ground.

These catches can also be taken one- and two-handed. A catch taken one-handed behind your head while leaping backwards is particularly useful in current Twenty20 games. Whether catching the ball one- or two-handed, the fingers need to be spread to create a big catching area.

Two-handed diving catch on the move

Note the great balance and position of the hands

HOW TO PRACTISE

Introductory level
With tennis balls or incrediballs, hit high catches in front, right, left and over the head of the fielder. Focus on moving to the ball quickly.

Intermediate level
As above, but with focus on working one specific area at a time, for example six catches to the left, six catches to the right. Extend the length and height of the hits through each set. Tennis-racket hits can be used to create real air-time on the ball.

Advanced level
With hard-ball hits, stretch the fielder with six rapid-fire high catches. As soon as one catch is taken strike another ball into a different area, forcing the fielder to move quickly to the next catch.

TROUBLESHOOTING

- Don't leave it too late to prepare your hands on approaching the ball.

- Don't take your eye off the ball.

- Call loudly to take the catch: collisions with other fielders are possible.

> **Fielding captain's note**
>
> A skied high catch can potentially go to any area on a cricket pitch, so work with the coach to make sure all the team practises high catches regularly.
> Highlight fielders who have particularly good hands in this skill and place them in the field where this type of catch is hit more often – in other words long-off and leg-side boundary.
> It's a simple skill to replicate so practise hard.

HIGH BOUNDARY FLICK-BACK CATCH

29.

HOW TO EXECUTE IT

Of all the new fielding innovations that Twenty20 has brought to the game, this is probably the newest and potentially most exciting. This is fielding at its best, with cricketers leaping and hanging in mid-air to catch one- and two-handed skied catches that are going for six over the boundary. It is clear that top professional teams are now practising this as part of their training programme.

The important thing is that with the fielder's momentum taking them over the boundary line, the ball must be flicked/thrown back in the air before they cross the line; this allows them a few seconds to stop, step back into play and take the catch.

A recent law change also states that the fielder's first contact with the ball must be when some part of his person is grounded within the boundary or, if he is airborne, that his final contact with the ground before touching the ball was within the boundary.

In the worst-case scenario this move saves runs, even if the catch is not ultimately taken.

As well as the obvious athleticism and catching skills required to perform this move, another important aspect is having the awareness of the space around

Catch taken within boundary...

...ball thrown back before crossing the line...

...fielder keeps eyes focused on ball while coming back into play...

...and takes the catch within the boundary

you – in particular you need to develop your peripheral vision when close to the boundary line.

HOW TO PRACTISE IT

Introductory level
Place a fielder holding a ball in a standing position alongside an imaginary boundary line. From this position throw the ball up into the air while taking a few steps at pace over the boundary line and then stepping back into play to take the catch.

Intermediate level
Now run towards the boundary line with a ball in your hands timing your throw into the air before you go over the boundary line. With your momentum taking you over the line stop as quickly as you can, allowing time to get back and hopefully take the catch. Practise this from different angles getting the required feel to master the skill.

Advanced level
High catches are now thrown or hit at different angles towards the fielder on the boundary who practises the skill in full.

The feed is important here, as you want to push the fielder's momentum towards the boundary line.

In some cases it may not be possible to take the catch and pop it up for a return catch; however, it will save four or six runs if it is thrown back into play. This is particularly relevant if the potential catch is right on top of the boundary line while taking a catch one-handed off the ground.

TROUBLESHOOTING

- Don't look to throw the ball back unnecessarily if you can take the catch and stop before the boundary line.

- Athleticism is a key component of performing this skill so work this area hard.

BACKING UP

30.

Backing up both at the wicketkeeper's end and bowler's end for overthrows is part and parcel of cricket, from the early stages of entering the game as a young cricketer through to the international arena.

In Twenty20, something as simple as backing up has been elevated to a new level, with fielders sprinting from the boundary – particularly outside of the powerplay overs – to cover an overthrow. Additionally it can put doubt into the batter's mind.

Another innovation, with a higher ratio of the stumps being thrown down, is that fielders are now backing up in pairs either side of the stumps to create an arrow-like formation, either behind the keeper or the fielder at the non-striking end. This covers the potential ricochet off the stumps if the batter has made his ground and is looking for the overthrow.

It is also worth mentioning at this stage that the positioning of the fielder at the stumps: they may be in front of the stumps to take the ball rather than the traditional place, behind the wicket. This is a personal preference with both options to be practised but will vary depending on how quickly you can get to the stumps and the direction from which the ball is thrown in.

PART FOUR

WICKETKEEPING

INTRODUCTION

A good wicketkeeper is particularly important in Twenty20 cricket, where one or two runs or a catch, stumping or run-out can mean the difference between winning or losing.

It is the perennial problem of coaches, managers and captains as to whether they play the wicketkeeper-batter or the out-and-out keeper. In a Twenty20 match the argument for the out-and-out keeper could be stronger than in any other form of the game.

A wicketkeeper who can expertly stand up to the stumps to most, if not all, of your bowlers during the course of the 20 overs can give your bowlers an important advantage in winning matches. It pins batters in their creases and denies them the opportunity to use their feet.

In this part we will look at standing up to the stumps to seamers and standing back, as well as other areas such as running batters out.

Standing up to the stumps

STANDING BACK 31.

It's important to realise that wickets are crucial at the top end of the innings. With the new ball that nips around, the keeper is always in the game with caught-behinds standing back.

At the beginning of the innings, the keeper will want to see if there is movement off the pitch which could bring the big edge caught-behinds into the game. Also towards the death, when the faster bowlers come on to bowl, you may also need to stand back.

Even if the keeper feels comfortable standing up, it's important to assess each batsmen for strengths and weaknesses. This may bring bouncers into play.

Lastly, at any time when a stroke like the Dilscoop is being used (see page 40), or some other kind of innovation, the keeper may need to stand back.

HOW TO DO IT

Twenty20 keeping standing back is almost like goalkeeping: the ball can go anywhere, so stand where you can access both the off- and leg-side, and be prepared to dive. Stand back at a distance where the ball will hit you just above the knee.

HOW TO PRACTISE IT

Introductory level
Stand with your feet shoulder-width apart, hands out in front, presenting a large target for the ball. Coaches should feed a tennis ball to the keeper at pace, at consistent height and width. Then move on to an incrediball. The keeper should focus on catching the ball with soft hands.

Intermediate level
The keeper should find a comfortable position where they can stay as low as

Looking to take the ball with soft hands

106 / PART FOUR: WICKETKEEPING

possible, but still be able to look straight ahead. Concentrate on taking the ball under your eyes or slightly towards your inside hip. Coaches should feed the ball with slightly more variation of height and width.

Advanced level

Loading the inside leg and powering off

The player should be ready to dive, load their inside leg ready to power off. They should look for variations the bowler might use, i.e. slower balls where a long barrier may be an option. A keeper may need to take their gloves off ready to throw the stumps down if the non-striker is looking to run to them, so practise taking balls one-handed as well. Practise against actual bowlers on the square.

TROUBLESHOOTING

- Watch the ball all the way in: don't raise your head or take your eyes off the ball too early.

- Give with the ball: you need soft hands to take the ball cleanly.

- Don't move too early.

- Come up with the bounce. If you come up too soon you may be too high to catch the ball.

> ### Fielding captain's note
>
> Your keeper has an invaluable view of what's going on, so use his observations to keep yourself a step ahead of the game. Discuss field placings and bowling changes with him.

STANDING UP TO THE SEAMERS

32.

Standing up is one of the most useful techniques used by modern keepers. In Twenty20 cricket the batter is looking for any advantage they can get, including running down the wicket and just having the freedom to leave their crease for an expansive shot. You can also cut off short singles if the batsman looks to drop and run. As an added bonus you are right at the stumps ready for a run-out.

If the batter is advancing down the wicket to hit the ball or if you get the feeling he is looking to do so, that is the time when you should be looking to move up to the stumps.

If the bowler feels comfortable with you standing up then it's sometimes worth being proactive and standing up from the start. Work closely with your bowlers to devise your plan of attack.

Stance standing up to the wicket: note hands close to the ground

Fingers pointing downwards, hands open to create a big target for the take

Effecting the stumping

HOW TO DO IT

Stand with your left foot just on off-stump if there is a right-hander facing, or with your right foot just behind off-stump if it's a left-hander facing. It's really important to go all the way down into a crouching stance so you can rise with the bounce of the ball.

HOW TO PRACTISE IT

Introductory level

The keeper should stand with feet shoulder-width apart facing down the wicket. Crouch down into the keeping position with hands on the floor. The coach should feed the ball to the keeper bouncing on a length; the keeper should take the ball just above knee height, watching the ball right into the gloves and giving slightly with their hands.

Intermediate level

The keeper begins in the same position. Now get the feeder to change the length of the ball so that some bounce higher and some pitch closer to the keeper's feet, e.g. half-volley. The keeper must keep their hands as low as possible so the ball doesn't skid under them. When they take the ball they should pretend to take the ball back to the stumps.

Advanced level

Practise taking the ball for a right- and left-hander using the same methods. You can also add a shadow batter to these drills. Ask someone to stand in front of the keeper with a bat pretending to hit the ball but missing. This will form the most realistic practice, as it creates the same sense of distraction as you get in the game.

TROUBLESHOOTING

- Don't come up too early.

- Watch the ball all the way in – you don't want to drop it and miss a catch or stumping.

- Move quickly with as little movement as possible so you can get back to the stumps for a stumping.

> **Fielding captain's note**
>
> When standing up to the stumps, the keeper has an almost identical view of the fielders as the batsman, so speak to your keeper to get the angle of the fielders right. Be aware as a captain, though, that with the keeper up at the stumps, fine leg and third man may have to come a bit straighter to cover small nicks and leg-byes.

PART FIVE

FITNESS

INTRODUCTION

With the advent of this shortened version of the game, cricket has become more high-profile and glamorous all over the globe. Many players have become A-list celebrities and their earnings have seen a huge increase.

Inevitably there is now enormous pressure on these athletes to perform consistently well, meeting the high expectations of their sponsors and backers. A great example of this is the IPL Twenty20 competition, which usually runs for six weeks during April and May.

As well as the simple increase in athleticism expected from players these days, they also need to be in supreme condition to perform at their optimal level day after day during a tournament like the IPL. And this doesn't come about without carefully designed training plans, close monitoring and testing, and a great deal of hard work on the part of the players and their coaches.

This section contains three chapters designed to help you get your team into peak physical condition. Chapter 33 describes four simple tests to help you monitor each player's level of fitness, and the results of their training. Chapter 34 contains some simple drills that enhance fitness, teamwork and awareness. And chapter 35 lists key exercises that Twenty20 players need to pratice to improve their strength and stamina, and prevent injuries.

> **Twenty20 program construction**
>
> With this form of the game being the most explosive, it is important to think about work/rest periods carefully when designing your program. Although athletes need adequate recovery time when training, try to keep this to the minimum – focus on keeping them working at their optimal rate and intensity for as long as possible. Training in this way means that when players are out in the arena performing, the actual game is so much easier.

PHYSICAL TESTING

33.

Before we start the tests, it is important to understand why we test the athletes – we are not simply testing them for the sake of it! Here are the four key reasons for testing:

1. Identify strengths as well as weaknesses
2. Monitor progress
3. Continual education for both the coaches and the athlete
4. Predict performance potential

We describe four simple tests in the pages that follow: vertical jump; sprint; run-a-three agility; and abdominal strength. These are fundamental areas to focus on when training for Twenty20 cricket. You can also develop your own tests to monitor the fitness of your players and the effectiveness of your training program. Whether using our tests or devising your own, it helps to understand the basic facts and stats of the Twenty20 game – this information should help you get to grips with the structure of any test.

> **Know the facts**
>
> 1. The distance between each popping crease is 17.68m
> 2. The distance between each bowling crease is 20.12m
> 3. The average time for an over to be bowled is roughly 3½ minutes
> 4. This equates to a ball being bowled every 35 seconds
> 5. A wicketkeeper squats a minimum of 120 times in one innings
>
> From nine IPL matches reviewed, average runs scored by the batsmen were as follows:
>
> a) 0s: 43%   c) 2s: 5%   e) 4s: 10%   g) 6s: 5%
> b) 1s: 37%   d) 3s: 0%   f) 5s: 0%   h) 7+: 0%

Whether you use the information above to devise your own tests or work with the tests in this book, remember these three rules:

- Make sure the tests are sport-specific.

- Have normative data to hand to compare the results (see below).

- Perform the tests regularly to monitor the results of your training.

- Most importantly, make sure someone – be it coach or captain – can interpret the data and devise a program that is relevant from the results of the tests.

NORMATIVE DATA

We have provided normative data with which to compare your results for each of the tests that follow. Please note that this relates to male Test cricketers and Sheffield Shield players – the Australian equivalent to county players in the United Kingdom.

Height and weight of players used for normative data

	Mass (KG)		Height (cm)	
Squad	Average	Range	Average	Range
Test Player	85.8	72.8–109.8	183.6	169.8–202.0
Sheffield Shield	79.9	62.9–103.2	182.7	174.1–208.9

Adapted, with permission, from P. Bourdon, B. Savage and R. Done, 2000, 'Protocols for the physiological assessment of cricket players'. In Physiological tests for elite athletes, *edited by the Australian Sports Commission (Champaign, IL: Human Kinetics), 239–42*

TEST 1: Vertical jump
Rationale: Leg strength and speed (power) are extremely important for all cricketers. These two attributes contribute to the speed and agility required for fielding, wicketkeeping and of course running between the wickets. This test is also vital for bowlers – it will help them monitor and practise their ability to absorb the forces experienced by the legs during a delivery.

Test procedure: The athlete stands side-on to a wall and reaches up with the hand closest to the wall, keeping feet flat on the ground. The point of the fingertips is marked and recorded, and this is called your *standing reach height*. The athlete then stands away from the wall, performs a countermovement and jumps up as high as he or she can, marking the wall with their fingertips at the highest point of the jump. This is called your *jump height*. The distance between your standing reach height and jump height is your recorded score. The test will conclude when the predetermined number of jumps has been recorded.

Parameters: Number of jumps: three with your best jump-height recorded.

Vertical jump test

Squad	Average (cms)	Range (cms)
Test Player	52.6	22–78
Sheffield Shield	54.8	38–69

Adapted from Bourdon, Savage and Done, 2000, 'Protocols for the physiological assessment of cricket players'.

TEST 2: Sprint

Rationale: In cricket, whether you are fielding or batting, the athletes must be able to accelerate over short distances and get from point A to point B in the quickest possible time.

Test procedure: With a tape measure to hand mark out 10-, 20- and 40-metre distances. Place a cone at the start, and to mark each of the three distances. The athlete stands behind the first cone and on the coach's command, sprints the 10-metre stretch a few times, before moving on to test the other distances.

Parameters: You do three sprints of each distance, recording your best time on each distance.

Sprint test

Squad	10m (speed in seconds)		20m (speed in seconds)		40m (speed in seconds)	
	Avge	Range	Avge	Range	Avge	Range
Batsman	1.78	1.70–1.86	3.04	2.82–3.19	5.42	5.08–5.65
Pace Bowler	1.76	1.75–1.79	2.99	2.88–3.07	5.30	5.17–5.49

Adapted from Bourdon, Savage and Done, 2000, 'Protocols for the physiological assessment of cricket players'.

TEST 3: Run-a-three agility

Rational: This test is ideal for cricketers to test their running speed between the wickets. It also provides important data on their turning speed, and helps identify which leg is stronger on push-off. When you turn to the right you are pushing off your left leg; the opposite applies when turning to the left.

Test procedure: Mark out the points for the test as per the diagram on the next page. The athlete stands with one foot behind the crease line at point A, with the cricket bat in hand. Please note that no hands should be touching the ground.

On the coach's command the athlete starts the test, running to point B. The stopwatch is started as soon as the athlete's back foot leaves the ground, and the test is stopped when the bat crosses the crease line (point B) at the end of the third run.

When the athlete passes through the cone at the 12.7-metre mark another stopwatch is started. After the athlete turns at the crease line and returns through the 12.7-metre mark the stopwatch is stopped with the time recorded. This is called your *turning speed*.

Parameters: Repeat the test four times, turning twice to the right and twice to the left. Record your best result.

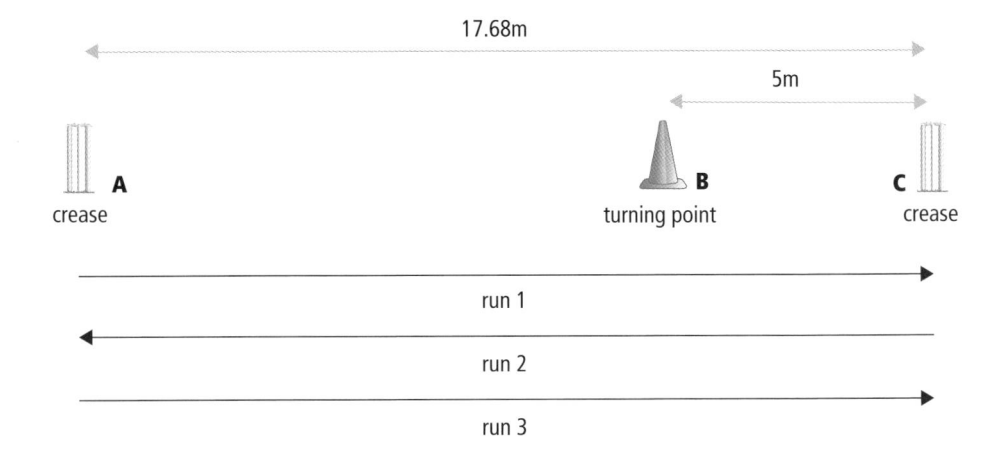

Run-a-three agility test

	Length speed (seconds)		Turn speed (speeds)	
Squad	Average	Range	Average	Range
Test Player	9.65	8.61–11.20	2.12	1.79–2.48
Sheffield Shield	9.32	8.68–9.99	2.16	1.86–2.39

Adapted from Bourdon, Savage and Done, 2000, 'Protocols for the physiological assessment of cricket players'.

TEST 4: Abdominal strength

Rational: Core strength/rigidity is of vital importance for cricketers. It's essential for power and plays a role in the prevention of injury. Good core-strength is required to generate rotational power for a batsman running between the wickets, for a fielder turning to throw back a ball, and to assist in power production when a bowler executes their delivery.

Test procedure: There are seven stages to this exercise, which all consist of varying forms of the sit-up. The first stage is the easiest, progressing up to a very challenging stage seven. Not all athletes will be able to attempt each stage, but with practice it will become easier. Note the scores achieved by professional players (see the table on page 120), and don't expect too much, especially from younger athletes!

Each athlete is allowed three attempts to pass each stage. All movements must be executed in a controlled manner. The player's score is the last stage completed successfully.

> **An attempt is *unsuccessful* if the player:**
>
> - Lifts either foot partially or totally off the floor
> - Throws the arms or head forward in a jerky manner
> - Moves arms from the nominated position
> - Lifts hips off the floor
> - Fails to maintain a 90° angle at the knee
> - Is unable to complete the nominated sit-up

Start position: The same for all stages. Lie on your back with your feet on the floor. Feet should be comfortably apart with a 90° bend at the knee.

Stage 1: Palms over knees. Arms straight with hands resting on thighs. Move forward until the fingers touch the knee.

Stage 2: Elbows over knees. Arms straight with hands resting on thighs. Move forwards until the elbows are touching the nee.

Stage 3: Forearms to thighs: Arms across and in contact with the abdomen with hands gripping opposite elbows. Move forward until the forearms touch mid-thigh.

Stage 4: Elbows to mid-thighs. Arms across and in contact with the chest with hands gripping opposite shoulders. Move forwards until elbows touch the mid-thighs.

Stage 5: Chest to thighs. Arms bent behind the head with the hands gripping opposite shoulders. Move forward until the chest touches the thighs.

Stage 6: Chest to thigh with 2.5kg mass. Arms bent behind the head with the hands crossed holding a 2.5kg mass. Move forward until the chest touches the thighs.

Stage 7: Chest to thigh with 5kg mass. Arms bent behind the head with hands crossed and holding a 5kg mass. Move forward until the chest touches the thighs.

Abdominal strength test

Squad	Average (stage)	Range (stage)
Test Player	4	3–5
Sheffield Shield	4	1–5

Adapted from Bourdon, Savage and Done, 2000, 'Protocols for the physiological assessment of cricket players'.

DRILLS

34.

What follows are some examples of drills you can devise that we believe will help your players perform at their optimum when playing this version of the game. You can run this with multiple athletes following each other down the course.

Think about specific rest times for your players. Keep them under pressure without pushing too hard. We have recommended a particular length rest-period after each set, to replicate the delay before the next ball in an over.

In due course you might want to think about progressions for each drill. For example, you can add push-ups at the end of a drill to create a more complex set. These will result in more complex and effective training drills.

DRILL 1. Zig-zag

Use cones to lay the zig-zag course, and place them five metres apart. The coach stands at point X. The players start at point A and sprint through the zig-zag course until they reach point B. At this point the coach will throw a ball to the player, who will catch it and throw it at the stumps. The athlete will then continue on their zig-zag course to point C, where the coach will now roll a ball along the ground towards them. The player attacks the ball and performs an underarm throw at the stumps. The athlete then sprints to the start and repeats the course.

Recommendation: Repeat the course four times and have a 30-second rest. This is one set. Do four sets in total.

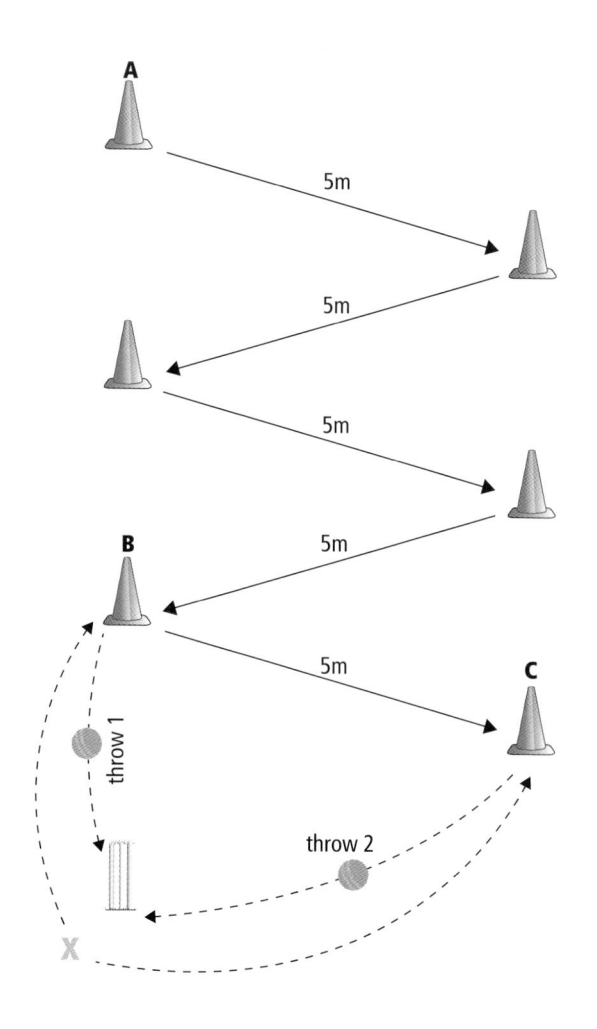

DRILL 2. **M-drill**

Use cones to lay an M-shaped course, placing them five metres apart. The coach stands at point X. The athlete starts at point A, running on the spot. The coach feeds a ball to the athlete who, upon receiving it, sprints through points B, C and D on the course. The aim is that the player is always facing forwards (in the direction of the coach at X); this will work their forward and back pedal-movement. When the athlete reaches point E, they throw the ball at the stumps. They should then side-step across to the start position, A.

Recommendations: Repeat the course three times, then have a 30-second rest. This is one set. Do five sets in total.

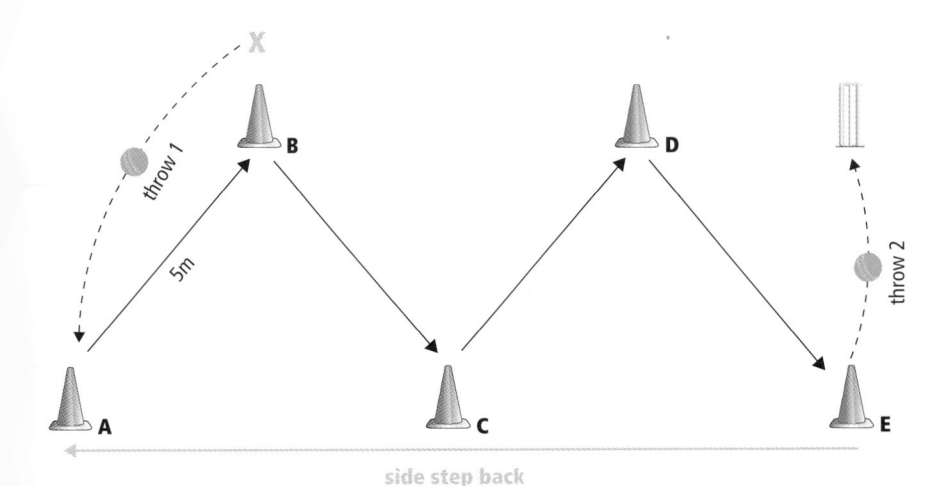

DRILL 3. **Bowling overload**

Practise on a real wicket, or use cones to mark out your distances (remember the distance between two batting creases is 17.68m). The bowler starts at their own predetermined bowling run-up point – say point A. Once they hit the crease, point B, they bowl the ball at the stumps. Then they need to complete their follow-through – for example, up to point C – and return to the start. From the delivery of the ball they have 35 seconds to get back to their predetermined run-up point and prepare to bowl the next ball.

Recommendation: 12 balls is one set. After each set have a two-minute rest and do four sets in total.

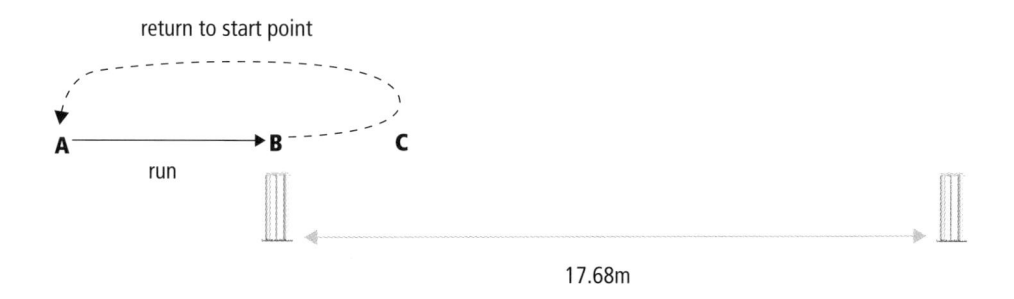

17.68m

DRILL 4. Running between wickets overload

Use a real wicket, or mark out the length of the crease (17.68m). The player starts with his bat inside the batting crease at A. At a signal, he sprints the length of the wicket, placing the bat inside the opposite batting crease at B, before turning to sprint back.

Each recommended set consists of the following:
- Run-a-three with 35-second rest. Repeat ten times. Take a three-minute rest.
- Run-a-two with a 35-second rest. Repeat ten times. Take a three-minute rest.
- Run ten singles with a 35-second rest between each. Finish.

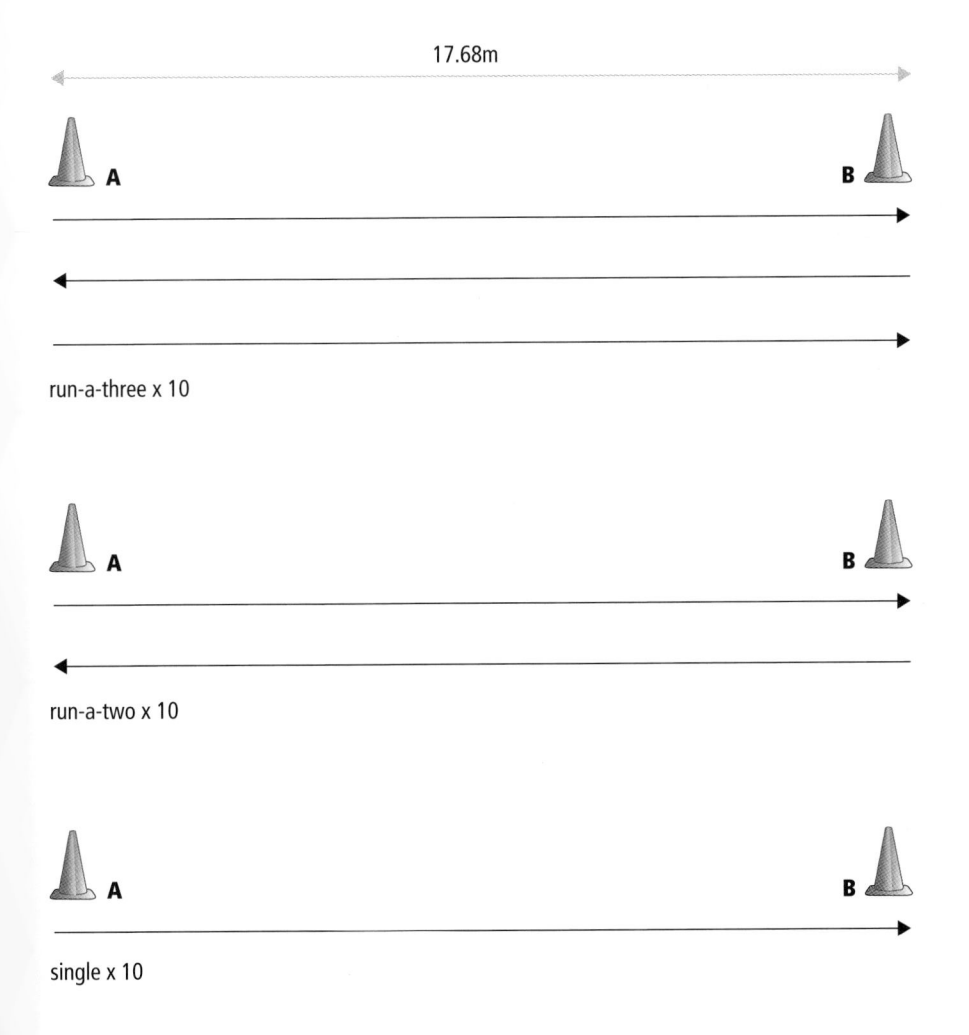

17.68m

A   B

run-a-three x 10

A   B

run-a-two x 10

A   B

single x 10

DRILL 5. **I-drill**

The cones are a minimum of five metres apart.

The player starts at the stumps with a ball in hand. They back-pedal to the centre cone (A), then side-step out to the left or right cone (B or C). When they reach the cone, they then throw the ball back at the stumps. Once completed they run back to the start (the stumps).

Recommendation: Repeat the drill five times (one set), then have a 35-second rest to recover. Do four sets.

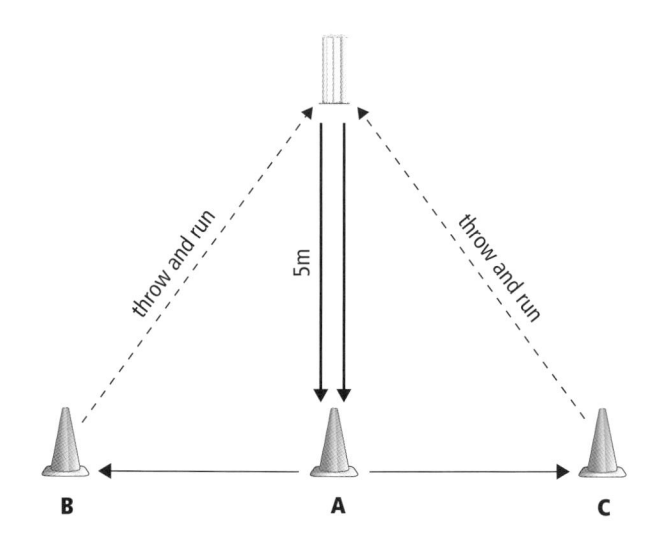

DRILL 6. W-drill

Use a ladder and some cones to set out the course.

The player starts at A. They sprint forward through the ladder, stepping in each hole. Once at the other side at B, the coach (placed at X) will throw a ball to the athlete. On the coach's command the player will then either break out to the right or left and run through the course (C, D and E), always facing forwards. On reaching the end they throw the ball at the stumps and return to the start position.

Recommendation: Completing the course four times equals one set. Then have a 35-second rest and repeat five sets.

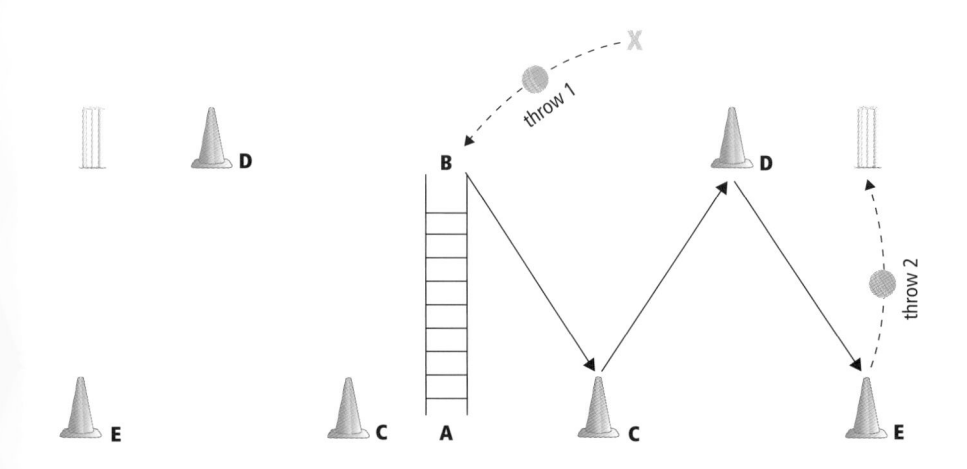

DRILL 7. **Shuttle run**

Lay out a course using cones at the following distance from your start position at point A: 5m, 10m, 20m, 30m and 40m. The player should sprint to the first cone and return to the start position, then sprint to the next cone and return to the start position, and so on.

Recommendation: Completion of the whole course as above equals one set. Rest for 35 seconds and do four sets. Your rest period between sets remains the same.

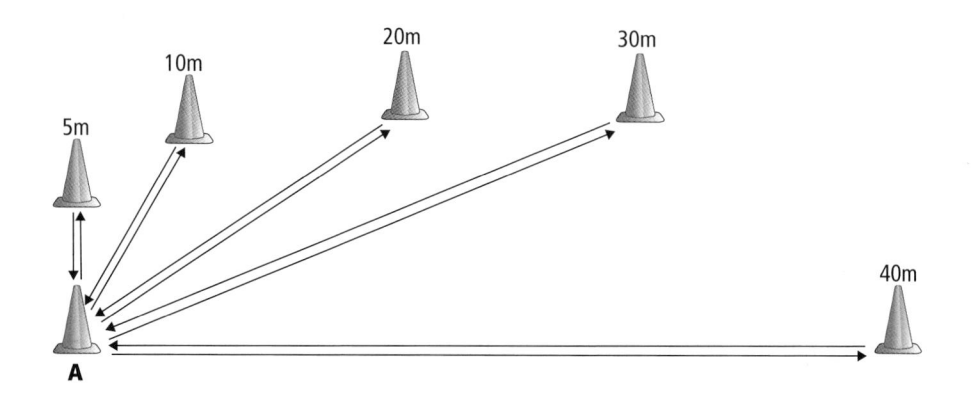

EXERCISES

CORE STRENGTH

The players should have great core strength/rigidity. This is important as the Twenty20 game means they are often forced to rotate at high velocities. This requires good balance and an extremely strong core. Below are three different sets of exercises to encourage the development of a strong core.

CORE CIRCUIT 1

When doing each of the six exercises in this circuit, make sure that all movements are done in a slow and controlled manner.

Recommendation: Do 20 repetitions of each exercise, alternating sides if appropriate. Once you have completed the circuit rest for one minute – this is one set. Do three sets in total.

1. Tuck crunches 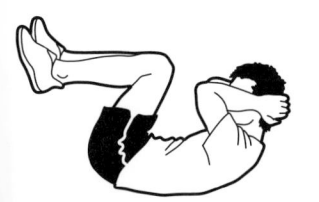
2. Oblique crunches 
3. Scissors 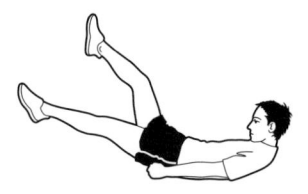
4. Toes touches 
5. Reverse crunches 
6. Bicycles

CORE CIRCUIT 2 – WITH MEDICINE BALL

These exercises utilise a medicine ball for added strength and conditioning. They are a great way of improving your core strength and preventing injury. Make sure that all exercises are done with controlled movements.

Recommendation: Do ten repetitions of each exercise, alternating sides if appropriate. Once you have completed the circuit rest for two minutes. This is one set; do five sets in total.

1. Sit-up throws

2. Oblique rotations

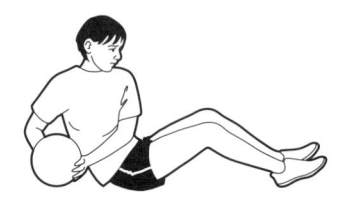

3. Side toe lunge

4. Around the clock

5. Reverse chop

6. Squat to overhead

CORE CIRCUIT 3 – WITH CABLE

The movements from start to finish are explosive. When returning to the start make sure it is done in a slow and controlled manner.

Recommendation: Do ten repetitions of each exercise. This is a set. Once you have completed one set, rest for one minute. Do four sets in total.

1. Cable chops

2. Reverse cable chops

3. Mid-core cable rotations

BALANCE

Being a good cricketing athlete requires great balance, especially if you have the ambition of being a world-class batsman. Below are some exercises that will help you achieve this goal.

BALANCE CIRCUIT 1 – WITH BALANCE BOARD

While performing these exercises, remember to keep your back straight at all times. To increase the level of difficulty, perform the exercises with no shoes. The use of the balance board means all your muscles will be working harder to keep you upright.

Recommendation: Do ten repetitions of each exercise, alternating sides as necessary. This is one set. Repeat three sets with a two-minute rest in between each.

1. Single leg squat with cone touch

2. Single leg lunge on to balance board

3. Side lunge on to balance board

4. High knee cross lunge on to balance board

BALANCE CIRCUIT 2

These are static exercises where you hold your position for a length of time. Remember to keep your back straight. It's important to engage your abdominals, pulling your tummy button into your spine at all times.

Recommendation: Hold each position for 30 seconds with a 30-second rest in between each. At the end of the circuit rest for two minutes. Do three sets of the circuit in total.

1. Reverse bridge

2. Reverse bridge single leg-raise

3. Bosu ball prone superman
   (you can also do this without the ball)

SHOULDER PREHABILITATION

This is a key area that requires continual attention to prevent bowling injuries. These exercises also rectify imbalances that naturally occur through overuse of one side of the body – relevant to nearly all fielders as well as to batsmen playing either left- or right-handed.

These exercises should be done every day to improve the overall strength of the shoulder girdle and, more importantly, the rotator-cuff muscles which hold the shoulder joint in place.

When performing all of these exercises, make sure that you keep your shoulder girdle in a neutral position. These exercises should all be done in a slow, controlled manner with real focus on isolating the area.

Recommendation: Do three sets on each. If it is a unilateral exercise complete three sets on each side.

1. Shoulder rotation with upper arm at 90% angle

2. Shoulder rotation with upper arm at 70° angle

3. Shoulder rotation with upper arm 0° angle

4. Reverse-fly with elbows slightly above the shoulder

5. Pull-down with elbows tucked into the ribs